Meaningful Matters

Reflections on Joy, Loss
and Our Changing World

9/21/2017

TO DR. THOMAS,

THANKS FOR HELPING ME

LEARN TO SPEAK MY LATENT CONVICTION.

Jeff Kelly Lowenstein

ISBN: 978-0-9886817-2-9 (Print)
ISBN: 978-0-9886817-1-2 (Mobi)

Publisher: Three Weddings Press
Design/Typesetting (Interior): Chris Moore www.fromprinttoebook.com

To Ginna with love and appreciation.

TABLE OF CONTENTS

"So, are you going to write about it on your blog?"

Fernando Diaz, December 2008

AN INTRODUCTION
BY DANNY POSTEL

"**I**'m talking about big stuff here," my friend Jeff Kelly Lowenstein writes in "Sources of Joy: The Many Gifts of an Abundant Life," one of my favorite chapters in this wonderful book.

Indeed he is. About 20 years ago my friend Scott Sherman gave me a copy of Norman Rush's novel *Mating*. In his inscription, Scott wrote that the book was about "all the things that matter most." That phrase resonated with me deeply and has stayed with me. The same could be said of this book of Jeff's essays. It deals precisely with all the things that matter most — friendship, ideas, mentors, movements, travels, trauma, family, politics, joy, books, relationships.

But the book's central theme, for me, is gratitude. Reading Jeff's marvelous reflections on life–first on his blog, and now collected here in book form–has taught me an enormous amount about being grateful.

It was reading an article by the anthropologist T. M. Luhrmann a few months back that really brought this into focus for me. Rituals, she wrote:

work, if by "work" we mean that they change people's sense of their lives. It turns out that saying that you are grateful makes you feel grateful. Saying that you are thankful makes you feel thankful... In a study in which undergraduates were assigned to write weekly either about things they were grateful or thankful for...those who wrote about gratitude felt better about their lives as a whole... There have now been many such studies.

There it was! This poignantly illuminated what I loved so much about Jeff's blog, particularly his "Sources of Joy" series and his tributes to various people–teachers, friends, authors, mentors–who have influenced him and his life. On myriad occasions Jeff's essays have given me pause and made me think about those figures in my own life. Who are the teachers, friends, authors, and mentors who have shaped my path? What do I owe them for the gifts they have given me? Have I ever expressed my gratitude to them?

Reading Jeff's essays left me with these questions, and inspired me to start writing in a more personal vein — something I had long resisted doing.

"I find myself drawing far more than before on my own experience to understand life's events, time's passage and current moments," Jeff writes (again in "Sources of Joy: The Many Gifts of an Abundant Life"). As do I. And it was reading Jeff that sparked this turn for me. His impassioned tributes to the figures who have made a difference in his life–the "lives we carry with us," in the felicitous phrase of the psychiatrist and moral philosopher Robert Coles (and how poetic that Jeff profiles Coles himself in one of this volume's finest chapters) have stirred me to reflect more deeply on the lives I carry with me. *On My Teacher's Shoulders*, Jeff's beautiful homage to his mentor Paul Tamburello, has made me think a lot about the many shoulders on which I stand.

And this, in turn, has made me a more grateful person. As Luhrmann notes, it's the *ritual* that can "change people's sense of their lives." On his blog, Jeff made a ritual of expressing gratitude to various people in his life. And the act of reading these expressions of gratitude itself became a ritual, an infectious one that in turn inspired tremendous feelings of gratitude. And for this—to come full circle—I am, and will always be, deeply grateful to Jeff.

As are many, many others. For reading Jeff's blog was very much a collective experience. The blog became a conversation piece among those of Jeff's readers who know one another offline. I often discussed Jeff's latest posts with Derrick Milligan, a mutual friend and devoted reader of the blog, at tennis practice. We bonded over our love of the blog. Others did as well.

But even those of us who have never met, and never will, are connected through the conversation Jeff conducted with us. A community of readers formed around the blog. Jeff's "Sources of Joy" became a source of joy for us.

Jeff's blog has colorfully chronicled his spirited journey and passionate engagement with the world. But it has done more than that–it has inspired its readers to make our own journeys more spirited and to engage the world more passionately.

This volume gives Jeff's reflections new life. With some of his very best pieces assembled here in book form, they will move many more of us. For those of us who read Jeff's blog faithfully, this "Greatest Hits" anthology is a real treasure. But this volume is more than a mere collection of blog posts. It is a bona fide book of essays, one with an elegant, even lyrical coherence. I hope it reaches the blog's loyal followers and many new readers alike.

"Believer in living with gratitude and joy," Jeff's Twitter bio reads. These essays give powerful expression to that credo. May they inspire this exquisite book's readers to live with gratitude and joy, or at least to strive to do so.

Thank you, Jeff.

Section I

JOY

FAMILY

LIFE LESSONS
FROM MOM AND RAFAEL

February 18th, 2012

Alice Lowenstein sits outside a hotel in Evanston.
(Photo by Jon Lowenstein/NOOR)

You might not think a young man from rural Mexico seeking his fortune in America and a middle-aged Jewish mother of three boys would have much in common, but physical devastation has a way of bringing out a shared humanity.

The Mexican gentleman in question is Rafael. My brother Jon and I met him five years ago during a project we did about undocumented Latino immigrants who became disabled on the job.

The middle-aged woman is my mother, Alice Adelman Lowenstein.

Both suffered accidents that had instant and permanent physical consequences.

For my mother, it was a car crash on a snowy President's Day in 1986.

And for Rafael, who had just arrived in this country with dreams of glory, it was a huge metal object falling on his back during his second week of work at a popcorn factory.

"My old life had ended," Rafael told Jon and me, in essence. "I had to accept that a new one had begun."

His words stunned me because Mom had used almost exactly the same language about her accident.

Both took a long time to adjust to their new realities.

Mom had to deal with physical changes and an inability to sleep through the night that continues until today.

In some ways, though, the most profound challenge for her was coming to terms with having sustained a massive closed head injury.

In the beginning, Mom spoke in ways that only made sense to people who had known her and understood the references she was making.

She could not handle too many stimuli like conversation switches and exposure to sunlight while talking.

She also had a very low frustration level.

Yet, through her own tenacity, her considerable financial resources, her access to some of the world's finest health care and the loving support of family, she gradually got better.

The improvement was not just physical and mental.

She came to have a different perspective on her life.

Rafael's new life came slowly, too.

He wallowed in depression and self-pity for most of a year before his uncle told him to get out of bed and into life.

His uncle did more than talk.

So did his brothers and his mother, all of whom moved here to support Rafael.

Rafael also had a dedicated lawyer outraged by what had happened to the young man. With the family's blessing, the lawyer pursued Rafael's case for years.

In the end, Rafael received more than $100,000 to purchase a home and car. For the rest of his life, he gets a monthly check of $1,200. For the first 20 years following the accident, Rafael receives additional annual payments of $15,000. The company paid for all of his medical bills for the first five years.

Gradually, he got stronger.

He started using his hands to propel a racing chair.

He learned how to use a computer.

His car was altered so that he could drive.

He also jumped out of a plane.

He did this, he said, not of any reckless, self-destructive urge, but rather to show himself that nothing was impossible.

Mom and Rafael expanded beyond themselves to give meaning to their personal struggles by helping others.

Mom created a non-profit organization and to this day works to support and encourage other people.

In the spring of 2007, Rafael joined dozens of other people with disabilities and thousands of other protesters at an immigration rights rally pumping their fists and chanting, "Los discapacitados no van estar discriminados!"

The people with disabilities will not be the victims of discrimination.

I don't want to paint an overly rosy picture.

More than a decade after his accident, Rafael's wound at being unable to marry and have children remained tender.

Mom still cannot sleep through the night and lost friends who were unable to make the transition to her new life.

But if this is true, so is it also true that we can all learn from their acceptance of the losses and embrace of the changes.

The message is not to be joyful that their accidents happened, but rather how to use dramatically changed circumstances to come to a different understanding of and attitude toward life.

Through their paths, Rafael and Mom have done that.

And for that I am grateful to both of them.

WEDDING TOAST TO MIKE AND ANNIE

Oct. 3, 2011

Mike Lowenstein and Annie Du walk toward their wedding reception
in October 2011 after stating their vows.
(Photograph by Jon Lowenstein/NOOR)

I've always known Mike.

We grew up together, sharing a room for the first 15 years of my life, playing for hours and hours across the street at Griggs Park, and enduring the shared indignity of Mom standing on the front porch, cupping her hands and yelling loud enough for the entire neighborhood to hear, "Michael, it's time to come in. You're Boy of the Day."

Mike has always had many gifts and positive qualities.

He's highly intelligent, possessing an omnivorous mind that can absorb quickly whatever he put in front of it.

He's a talented athlete: coordinated, strong, fast, and ferocious. I still remember seeing his eyes burn with intensity as he went for and got rebound after rebound over larger and seemingly stronger opponents.

He was fearless, unafraid to go for what he wanted without hesitation.

Mike is very loyal to his friends whose attendance today is tribute to the care he has shown each of them.

He also has an ability to formulate a strong opinion and argue for it very forcefully.

Beyond these gifts and qualities, Mike has always been clear about the central importance of family.

Even though our mutual assertiveness, Mike's legal training and more than a decade of practice can make for some heated discussions, there has never been any doubt that he cares about family.

Deeply.

He doesn't only care. He takes action based on his feelings.

When I ran the Boston Marathon as a fundraiser in honor of my former fourth grade teacher in 1999, Mike was there to help bring me home the last 4.2 miles.

Along with Jon, he was there as my best man when Dunreith and I got married in Look Park in July 2011.

He was there when my father-in-law died last year, even as he was doing yeoman duty on the frontlines when Mom was struggling with congestive heart failure.

I want to talk for a minute about that experience because, while Mike has had many gifts, being immediately decisive is not one of them. Anyone who has been around Mike for even a brief amount of time knows that making decisions about where to eat or what to order once there is not exactly a linear process.

As a result, it's not a huge surprise that Mike did not rush to get down on one knee, and, just before a double rainbow rose in the Grand Canyon, present Annie with a diamond ring.

He may see it differently. But I believe that the often lonely vigil he kept for days and weeks and months at Mom's hospital bed and apartment in

Brookline, advocating for her over and over again and nursing her back to health, helped him get over the hump and onto his knee.

Thank goodness he did.

I remember when my Aunt Helen first met my wife Dunreith when we were dating.

Her comment afterward to me was, "Whatever happens with you two, she's a fine woman."

What she meant was, "Please don't blow this, Jeff."

We all felt the same way about Annie.

Like Mike, Annie has many gifts–intelligence, a facility in languages, a deep understanding of literature, and a strongly developed visual sensibility.

But what most stood out for me about Annie was her warmth, her balance, her sense of humor, her generosity of spirit, her zest for travel and her excitement about the world.

She also has patience and, like Mike, a profound love of family.

Last December we met Annie's parents, Min Wen and Shan Shan, and got a sense of the home, values and tradition in which she had been raised. During the past couple of days we have had the privilege of meeting and getting to know her brother Bowei and his lovely wife Ann.

We said then, and we say again, how excited we are to meet them, how glad we are they are part of the family and how eager we are to develop our relationship through Annie and Mike in the months and years to come.

From 1995 to 1996 I lived in South Africa.

While there I attended several weddings and learned a Zulu song that people sing about the bride when they approve of her. It begins, "Umakoti Ngowethu, siyavuma," and it means, "Our bride. We agree."

I'd like to ask your help in singing the song now.

Mike, we're glad you decided.

Annie, we're enormously grateful you waited and agreed to marry our brother.

We are here for you.

We are thrilled for you.

We love you.

AVA KADISHSON SCHIEBER'S SOUNDLESS ROAR

Jan. 12, 2009

Ava Kadishson Schieber in her Chicago apartment in the fall of 2015. *(Photograph by Jon Lowenstein/NOOR)*

April 1941 was a dire time for Ava Hegedis.

She and her family had moved from Novi Sad, a small city about 50 miles north of Belgrade, to the Yugoslavian capital to escape the Nazi regime that had waltzed through her homeland in a week.

Her father Leo, a gifted amateur violinist, saw through the Nazi assurances of safekeeping for his and other Jewish families. Leo told his family the only way they could survive was to split up.

And so, having just turned 15 years old, Ava went to live in a farming village with relatives of her older sister Susanna's fiancé.

Her home was a small wooden structure between the family's pigsty and chicken coop.

Her possessions: art supplies that she managed to stretch and make last for 18 months and a 17-volume, leather-bound German language encyclopedia she lugged over the course to several trips through the woods to her former home.

Because she was educated, Ava had to pretend that she could neither hear nor speak.

To speak would reveal her accent, her education, her outsider status and her Jewishness.

To speak would mean death for her and her hosts.

So she pretended she was deaf and mute.

For four years.

After the war, Ava discovered that her father and sister had been killed. Her mother, who had survived, had been shattered by her experience and the loss of her husband and daughter.

After the war, too, Ava also realized that she would never belong in Communist-era Yugoslavia. In 1949 she abandoned a career in art, broke off a two-year relationship with a lover, signed over the deeds to her two houses and moved with her mother to Israel.

Ava tells the story of her family, her survival and her departure to Israel in *Soundless Roar: Stories, Poems and Drawings*, a fascinating and gripping book that haunts, challenges and inspires.

Full disclosure: Ava is a cherished family friend.

As the title suggests, *Soundless Roar* is replete with contradictions. During World War II and after, the comfortable existence she had known in the years before the Nazi takeover was utterly uprooted and torn asunder.

Ava recounts her story roughly in chronological order through the tales, which tell of her being her grandfather's "bundle of morning joy," taking the reader through her years in hiding and ending with her departure in 1949 for Israel.

But *Soundless Roar* is much more of a multi-layered and interconnected set of expressions than a simple relaying of her wartime experience, as valuable as those accounts are from any genocide survivor.

Taking place in a world where farm animals were better and closer companions than humans, the stories are filled with intimacy formed of alienation, with the aching longings of an unlived adolescence and with the haunting memories that Ava has continued to grapple with in the more than 60 years since the war ended.

At the end of the story "Trapped," for instance, Ava writes about the combination of fragmentary memory and moments of insight that has been her condition since the war:

"One feels as though one is hanging in the air, while elements around us in turmoil. At those times I would identify with bats, which try to survive in the invisible existence of darkness, hiding and silent. The Nazi era killed 6 million people. It maimed us survivors for life."

Many stories in the book are drenched in pain and hunger for the knowledge that will permit closure. Ava describes in the story "Spirits" how she and her mother desire to find out conclusively that Susanna would never return. Her mother chooses always to hope, but Ava comes to accept the reality of her sister's death.

She closes the piece with the following:

"I would have loved to have possessed the firm Buddhist faith and conviction to trust messages from the mountaintops that would be carried by the winds for my sister.

I still would."

The short sentences, the invoking of another faith tradition, the connection with nature and the admission of enduring uncertainty and longing contained in those two sentences give *Soundless Roar* much of its power and resonance.

The stories also explore how wartime memories can be activated many years later by seemingly mundane experiences. In "Ride into the City," a cab ride from an airport terminal in a nameless city brings Ava back to the war so vividly that she is drawn back to the war. In this case, the driver's head reminds her of a young man's head as he was pushed into a deadly black car and toward his certain death.

She ends the story:

"He did not turn toward. I remained safe. That whole event probably took seconds; it hounded me for years."

Again, one sees in the conclusion the tenuous hold Ava has on the current world, how quickly she can be plunged back into her wartime situation. Her awareness and uncertainty about the precise duration of the incident and the continual nature of both her original experience and the cab ride that triggered the potent memories are visible as well.

It is important to be clear, though, that *Soundless Roar* is not the work of a broken woman, nor are the stories the only element in the book.

Indeed, in many cases, loss is matched by memory, death by survival, absence by presence and destruction is met with creativity and resilience.

Ava's sketches merit attention, too.

Drawn in shadowy lines, the one before the story "Diary" shows a young child holding a limp toy in its right hand and the hand of an adult figure–possibly a parent?–in the left. The child's face evokes a Picasso-like head, with uneven facial features and two mouths that turn toward each other. There, as in the stories, connection, disconnection and loneliness course through the image.

The child's hand is reaching out and met by the larger figure, but warmth is absent from the holding. Similarly, the toy, perhaps a doll, which should be a source of pleasure, dangles loosely and in a parallel relationship to that of the child and the adult.

The poems, which also precede each story, have their own potency.

The title poem, for instance, captures the inadequacy of language, the disorientation caused by the apocalyptic event, the fragmentary nature of life and memory and the necessity for each person to decide for herself life's meaning:

soundless roar the title says
construct your own meaning from the image
of mute din
where a vague maze of lines
limited by size and form
just indicates the space it evolved from
no place to fit a key
mind must break open closed entry
and cross the threshold
stare into obscurity of revealed insight
face glare of unfeigned depths
and then the way back to innocence
has lost all road signs
hence time is nameless too
and word's abundant treasure inadequate
even with novel terms

Other survivor accounts have mined the themes that Ava explores in her work. The poetry's lack of periods and possibly circular structure evoke Dan Pagis' *Written in Pencil in a Sealed Boxcar*. Ava's pictures of children in a shattered world and the impossibility of its reconstruction are also dominant themes in much of Samuel Bak's work. And Elie Wiesel's *Night* tells a harrowing story of child survival in Auschwitz–Ava makes it clear that she was in the antechamber of hell, but not in hell itself.

But few books of any genre or period bring each of these elements together in a single work and with such thought-provoking intensity, insight and wisdom. If Ava's survival cannot be easily packed into a narrative of hope, neither can *Soundless Roar* be described as a cathartic exercise by a destroyed woman.

Wounded yet intact, Ava demonstrates remarkable resilience through her survival and her efforts, however admittedly imperfect, to render her experience with the range of tools at her disposal. While neither a comforting nor a straightforward work, *Soundless Roar* is unflinchingly honest in its recounting of her life before, during and after World War II. The book sounds a clarion call to the reader not to live by empty slogans like "Never Again," but to continually forge meaning in a chaotic, contradictory and often dangerous world.

We are the richer for Ava's survival and her work.

(Photograph by Jon Lowenstein/NOOR)

SOURCES OF JOY: DAN MIDDLETON

Feb. 22, 2012

Dan Middleton in the summer of 2015.
(Photo courtesy of Dan Middleton)

Sometimes it really is true that your life can change in a second.

Dear friend Dan Middleton learned that firsthand 30 years ago today.

A junior at St. Paul's School in Concord, New Hampshire, he had stayed up all night finishing an issue of the school's newspaper.

He was taking his second ski run on the day when he fell.

At first the fall didn't seem too bad, he thought.

But then he realized he couldn't move.

At all.

So he lay there on an early Monday morning, the chill spreading inside him matching the cold of the mountain as he understood that everything from then on would be different.

Another skier came over to Dan and asked him how he was doing.

Common courtesy on the slopes, this gesture might have saved his life.

This was not just any skier, but rather a doctor.

When he heard what had happened, the doctor told Dan instantly to lie still.

Thrashing about or trying to stand up–normal reactions under the circumstances–could have resulted in even more damage, or even his death.

Dan was taken down the mountain and to the hospital, where his medical ordeal began.

Months of traction followed.

Dan was unable to do anything but stare at the ceiling, grit it out through another day.

He came to accept the immense changes in his body that left him unable ever to walk again and his hands barely able to open a door.

He somehow made it back to St. Paul's, where he directed a play his senior year and was largely helped by classmates.

We met during our freshman year at Stanford.

Dan eventually became one of my closest friends.

We spent hours each night talking, watching the news, ordering pizza, and listening to music.

Hailing from a storied blue-blood lineage, Dan was pure Hudson Valley with a deep mellifluous voice, remarkable mimicry skills, and an incisive sense of humor with an uncanny ability to find the richest nugget.

He had known suffering from even before his accident, and thus has always listened to other people's travails with compassion and understanding and without judgment.

Dan helped me edit my columns and senior thesis about Dr. King, cleaning up sentences that read, "King was very popular with the other students. A fellow student pulled a gun on King."

We graduated 25 years ago this June. After the ceremony, he joined Mom, Jon, Mike and me as we had a celebratory frozen yogurt.

We've not seen each other much during these years–the last time we were together in person was 1997–but Skype has been a real boon to our relationship.

At various points, Dan's focused his considerable intellect and obsessive attention to detail on different literary masters. The past four years he's poured himself into politics.

Talking with him is like attending a seminar in real time as he unleashes a torrent of information, policy and media analysis.

As we talk, the conversation flows seamlessly between our freshman year antics, the latest sporting developments, family and other questions of the day.

Each time we speak Dan lifts my spirits by reminding me of our connection and my great fortune to have him in my life.

It very easily might not have been so, had he moved just that little bit before the doctor approached him after the fall on the ski slope that altered everything.

STEVE KANTROWITZ'S BOOK ARRIVES (AND SO DOES HE)

Sept. 7, 2012

Steve Kantrowitz celebrates his fiftieth birthday with his daughter Sophie
and longtime friend Tim Tyson.
(Photo courtesy of Jeff Kelly Lowenstein)

You know that feeling when a big, juicy package greets you after a full day at work?

That tingling of anticipation to see what the person has to say after toiling in the vineyards for weeks and months and years?

I had that in spades this evening.

That's because after biking home I found childhood friend Steve Kantrowitz's *More Than Freedom: Fighting for Black Citizenship in a White Republic, 1829-1889* sitting in an envelope on the dining room table.

I'm confident the work is headed for serious acclaim.

Eric Foner, one of the deans of American history, has already given it a very strong, if not glowing, review in *The Nation*. One of the highest marks of praise was Foner's favorable comparison of Steve's work with that of Bancroft and Pulitzer Prize winner Steve Hahn's book written a decade earlier.

Speaking of Hahn, he's one of two Bancroft winners whose endorsement appears on the back cover of Steve's book. (Aaron Douglas' evocative *Aspects of Negro Life: From Slavery to Reconstruction* graces the front.)

You've heard it here first.

I'm optimistic that Steve's book will get strong consideration for this kind of recognition.

As thrilling as that is, that's not the only reason I'm excited about Steve's work.

Any book is a tremendous accomplishment.

This one, which casts its gaze to the North with an insistence that the American story can only be fully understood by looking at pre- and post-Civil War, has the potential to expand our collective understanding of our nation's past.

Beyond that, it also represents Steve's emergence into the kind of thinker and historian we always knew he could become.

That's saying a lot.

After all, we first met 35 years ago.

We were both in All-Town Band–he played trombone, while I tooted away on the clarinet and bassoon–and we both participated in *Sixth Sense*, a townwide literary magazine.

Then in his science fiction phase, Steve wrote with a depth and sophistication that far exceeded my own or that of anyone else in the anthology.

Even then, it was apparent the boy had chops.

When we were applying to college, our senior English teacher, Margaret Metzger, gave Steve one of the strongest recommendations ever in her more than 30 years of teaching.

"If you don't take him, I don't know what you expect American public education to produce," she wrote, in essence, in her closing to Steve's early application letter to Yale.

He got in.

Steve spent about a year after college in the Bay Area, but we always knew he was headed for academia.

He did just that, winning a Mellon Fellowship to study at Princeton.

While there, he wrote his dissertation about Pitchfork Ben Tillman, the cantankerous and rabble-rousing South Carolinian governor and senator who both expressed and played a key role in shaping what Steve called the reconstruction of white supremacy.

Five years later, after snagging one of the best available history professorships that year, a post in Madison, Wisconsin, he published that work through the University of North Carolina press.

It was a creative book, yet one could feel, particularly in the initial chapters, Steve going through the required tasks of demonstrating that he had read and understood what others had written before him before he started to spread his own intellectual wings.

This newest work has no such hoops for him to jump through. Instead, it's a launch right into the guts of his subject–a look at black Boston and the interactions between white abolitionists and black Bostonians, a number of whom were former slaves.

On a profound level, Steve is looking into the question of what happens after a major victory in a freedom struggle.

Steve's plugged away at this work for at least a decade, laboring through a Bunting year at Radcliffe, the decline and death of his younger brother Jeff, falling in love with his eventual wife Pernille, and becoming a father to her boy Elliot and their daughter Sophie.

There was a period after several of our friends had gotten married when Steve and I would call each other and say, with half-joking anxiety, "We're behind!"

Over time, we've learned even more than we knew before that each of us is on our own path.

We also have, through our choices of single mothers, jumped ahead of those whom we felt we had trailed.

With this book, Steve has arrived at a higher level of intellectual maturity, judgment and potential influence.

One of the greatest treats in life for me is knowing family and friends over time, watching the journeys of our lives unfold, and making the connections between what happened so many years ago and where we have now taken ourselves.

The timing of Steve's book coming together and its publication could not be more auspicious.

Shortly after holding it lovingly and starting to read the first few pages, I watched the Democratic National Convention with Dunreith.

John Lewis, the fearless warrior for justice, talked about the Freedom Rides he participated in in 1961, the year Barack Obama was born.

Now in his 70s, Lewis said that we are a different country now than we were then, and pointed to Obama's election in 2008 as evidence of that change.

Yet, as the president and several other speakers noted throughout the evening, the work of full citizenship is not yet done–especially when one holds up the standard and vision that members of Boston's black community held of a citizenship of the heart, not just the law.

It is true that this task is not, and may not ever, be completed.

But it is also true that through his diligence, research, and bold, synthesizing analysis and interpretation, Steve has pointed us toward a different understanding of the national citizenship project that can inform how we see the present moment and the future ahead.

M. DAVID LEE III TURNS 47

Sept. 21, 2012

M. David Lee III looking sharp at age 47.
(Photo courtesy of M. David Lee III)

From the moment I met him in Mr. Tamburello's fourth grade class in September 1974, M. David Lee III, better known as "Scooter" to those of us who knew him when, has always known his own mind and carved his own path.

Let's start with his name.

How many kids do you know who had the confidence, no audacity, to make their first name an initial, include their line in the Lee lineage and insist that teachers and peers use the full package?

Then there were the sports teams.

We all loved the Celtics. Scooter was with the Philadelphia 76ers.

We were Patriots fans. Scooter supported the Dolphins.

And, in perhaps the biggest source of friction, we lived and died with the hometown Boston Red Sox.

Scooter openly and fervently rooted for our archrivals, the New York Yankees.

He wore a dark blue Yankees batting helmet. When we played stickball at the Pierce playground or on Cypress Street, he batted left-handed and constantly called out the form of his hero, "Reginald Martinez Jackson."

Scooter chose unusual sports to play, too. He joined the gymnastics team at Brookline High School, earning a varsity letter as a freshman.

Scooter's self-direction extended beyond athletics to politics and other arenas. He was the one who first told me about Malcolm X and said that his birthday should be a national holiday.

He would refuse to stand for the national anthem because he believed the country had not lived up to its creed of liberty and justice for all.

This took guts.

Kids would snicker and make fun of Scooter for taking his stand, or, more precisely, his decision to not stand.

The mockery got to Scooter.

Sometimes he'd start crying.

But he never stood up.

He did stand up to people he felt had wronged him, though.

Many of us would make the mental calculus of the costs of standing up to the bigger kid who cut in line or who made an unkind comment or otherwise broke the rules or violated someone's dignity.

Not Scooter.

He'd fight anyone.

Scooter didn't always win the battles, but he never shied away from them, either.

He carved a distinctive high school career.

In high school he won a Sophomore of the Year contest and spent the summer in Japan. He liked it so much that he spent the entire first semester of senior year there, too. While there, he participated in, and won, a national version of the Gong Show.

Beyond his independent set of choices, Scooter's always brought an enormous amount of charisma to all of his social interactions. His mix-ins at Steve's Ice Cream as the "Samurai Scooper" were things of legend.

He knew virtually everyone in high school.

At times, he would seem to be everywhere, playing drums in the marching band while quarterbacking the team.

When the school instituted a democratic form of government, Scooter campaigned on a pledge to bring Walkmans to Brookline High School.

After winning the election, he made good on his promise.

I ran head on into that charm when he and I competed to be the senior speaker at our graduation.

To be fair, Scooter engaged in a bit of gamesmanship, arranging for us to meet at late night hangout International House of Pancakes at midnight and not showing up at the appointed time.

By the time I realized he was not showing, my sleep was shot for the evening.

But to put his victory on my fatigue would take away from Scooter's uncanny ability to woo the crowd.

I still remember vividly waiting my turn, hearing the crowd roar at his comments, and writing, "He's taking it. He's taking it."

He did.

We were together at his father's house on 50 Waverly Street when the call came from the school telling him of his deserved victory.

We were on the opposite side of that contest, but were teammates every time we played our annual football game with our crew against his brother Teo, my brother Mike and their buddies.

We generally played the day after Christmas.

In a tribute to the surfeit of college bowl games, we called ours, "The Toilet Bowl."

We played 14 times between 1979 and 1996.

By the time we had stopped, the contest had shortened from two out of three games to the first team to seven touchdowns.

We had shifted from tackle to hard touch.

And we had even seriously considered Teo's suggestion of changing the game's name to the "No Benefits Bowl." ("Take it easy on the guys who have no benefits," he had declared in our yearly pre-game rules discussion at mid-field.)

Scooter somehow blended his charm and independence in a memorable wedding toast to Teo and his wife Sylvia, spending a good 75 percent of the speech talking about the Toilet Bowl victory tally-we won 12 games, while Teo's squad took two of the contests. Even while brandishing the trophy in

Teo's face, he still managed to pull off a heartfelt sigh from the crowd by eventually turning his attention to the newlyweds.

That's talent.

Celebrating after another Toilet Bowl victory.
(Photo courtesy of M. David Lee III)

These are all important examples of Scooter's character and nature, and perhaps the most autonomous part of his path began when he was in sixth and seventh grade. We can give George Lucas a lot of the credit for that.

It was in the summer of 1977 when the first *Star Wars* film was released.

Scooter saw it over and over and over.

But he wasn't just a spectator.

Watching the film and seeing the special effects let him know what he wanted to do with his life.

He's been pursuing that passion ever since. I had the privilege of being in one of Scooter's first films, playing the Han Solo character in *War with the Stars*. (It may seem hard to believe, but Mom's bowl cuts did give me a certain resemblance to Harrison Ford at that time.)

It's been many years since I've seen it, and, if I remember correctly, my saying, "Let's go!" is the only audible line.

Scooter's developed his talent in the nearly 30 years since we graduated from high school.

He's chased his dream through broadcasting and teaching jobs in Tennessee, Washington, D.C. and California.

He's done his filming in condensed bursts and done the editing in the post-work hours at home.

In 2005 Dunreith, Aidan and I traveled to Memphis, where Scooter hosted us in style at his home at Rancho Lago Mirage. He gave us a private screening of *DogMe: Potluck*, a film he made according to the avant-grade principles articulated by Danish directors Lars von Trier and Thomas Vinterberg.

We cut the showing short after deciding that the content was a tad inappropriate for Aidan, and we're looking forward to seeing it again soon.

Scooter's also been a loving father to Sage, his talented daughter who just matriculated at the University of Redlands in Redlands, California.

Our bodies show the signs of the nearly four decades since we first met.

None of our grandparents are still alive, although, very fortunately, all of our parents are.

In addition to having college-age children, we are still trying to make our mark on the world with the work we love.

Although we don't get together as often as we'd like–I last saw Scooter in December, when he came to Chicago for his maternal grandmother's funeral–the lack of contact doesn't make the gratitude I have for what Scooter's brought to my life any less profound. If anything, it only makes me treasure our friendship even more and heighten my anticipation for the times we will continue to share together.

THE MIXTURE OF LIFE: A TRIBUTE TO DAVE RUSSELL

June 4, 2011

Dave Russell with some of his students from the McKinley School in 2015. (Photo courtesy of Dave Russell)

It's been six days since I've put keyboard to blog, and it feels real good to be back.

I know I've written before about feeling like I am in the middle of life.

I've been relishing Aidan's increasing moves toward independence. In the past three weeks, he's attended his prom, gone to freshman orientation at Tulane, graduated and had a memorable road trip to Bonnaroo, a four-day music festival in Tennessee from which he thankfully returned. At the same time, I've been feeling the pain of my mother-in-law starting radiation treatment to deal with an inoperable brain tumor.

Yet events in recent days have reminded me anew that we have no idea how long we will live, and thus do not know which stage of life we are in, other than what doctor and author Spencer Johnson calls "the precious present."

To wit:

A childhood friend shared with me this morning that his wife, who is in the first half of her 40s, has had Parkinson's disease for the past two years.

I spoke tonight with a friend who is in her 50s and looking to get round-the-clock help for her 92-year-old mother.

And dear friend, dedicated teacher and personal hero, Dave Russell, had his own brush with mortality after encountering some heart difficulty.

All apparently went well with Dave's angioplasty and the insertion of a stent. It sounds like he should be able to travel to see one of his daughters in Chile in two short weeks. Still, a trip to the emergency room that results in learning about extensive heart valve blockage is hardly reassuring stuff.

I don't want just to explain Dave's medical condition, but rather to take some time and space to write about this extraordinary man who has been both mentor and friend to me during the 20 years since we first met on a chilly winter morning while waiting for the ferry to take us to Boston Harbor's Thompson Island.

The son of a school superintendent in Gardner, Dave is one of eight siblings. A fine student and athlete, he graduated from Amherst College in the late 70s. Many of his classmates went on to pursue and achieve financial success in fields like medicine and law.

Dave could have done that, too.

Instead, he became a union organizer at Massachusetts General Hospital for eight years, tenaciously pursuing his goal of helping the workers there gain collective bargaining rights.

Again, after that campaign ended without the final victory he had sought, he had a choice.

He moved into education.

Urban education, to be precise.

After getting his teaching credential and working in a few different settings, Dave got hired at Mckinley School in Boston's South End in 1988.

He's still there.

McKinley is a designated special education school in Boston's South End neighborhood.

On Thompson Island, where Dave and I first worked together and began our friendship, the students were part of a multi-agency program. Our goal was to get them into good enough shape so that they could take the ferry to the mainland to attend the "regular" Special Education school in the South End.

Our students were living on the island after having been removed from their homes due to some combination of physical, emotional and sexual abuse.

They also were in the throes of adolescence, and, in many cases, profoundly learning disabled.

Sometimes, when I would get frustrated with the students' behavior and my inability to get them to respond to my instruction, I would read their files.

They made me weep.

One girl did not know when she was born.

Another had been prostituted by her mother.

One boy had lost both parents to AIDS and had a fierce love for his younger brother.

Another waited in vain over and over again for his mother to pick him up and take him home for the weekend, as she had promised.

She rarely did.

Needless to say, the work was enormously challenging.

But Dave never gave up then, and he hasn't done so since.

He keeps bringing the same tireless efforts toward his students' academic and personal growth he had when he first arrived a quarter-century ago.

Yet in some ways the true measure of Dave's commitment can be found is the continual deepening of his teaching practice.

Dave's attended dozens of workshops on topics ranging from science to reading to history. He's led writing seminars for teachers for years.

He takes annual trips with his students to college campuses because he wants them to know he believes they can and will get there. We're not just talking about Roxbury Community College, even though that is one regular stop on the college tour circuit. Dave and his students have gone to Harvard Yard, too.

He's expanded his students' horizons by traveling to Africa and setting up communication between his charges and the young people in Ghana he's met.

In short, he's dedicated his considerable energy, talent and heart throughout his adult life in the service of his noble ideals of working to show some of Boston's most disenfranchised young people that they are witnessed, cherished and can succeed.

It's grueling work that can often be demoralizing.

Dave knows all too well the grim numbers about the dark fates that come to so many of his students, many of whom have ended up in prison or dead.

He has kept going and going, training a generation of teachers in his classroom and modeling teaching excellence for his colleagues throughout the building.

Now this jolting news.

I hope and believe what the doctors have told Dave is true.

Still, his health scare has been yet another reminder to me to savor the moments that make up a life, not because we know ours will eventually end, but because each day possesses many gifts and richness within it if we are open to receiving them.

UBER-CONNECTER DANNY POSTEL HEADS TO DENVER

Oct. 2, 2012

Danny Postel with Amina, a displaced Syrian child he helped teach basketball
in Turkey through the Zeitouna program in June 2014.
(Photograph by Mohamad Ojjeh)

With some people, you only talk about specific topics.

It can be sports or politics or family or weather or personal history.

Venturing beyond those boundaries can lead to discomfort or silence or both.

Then there are the friends with whom the conversation is about one subject: life.

Everything flows from and into that central, ongoing, shared, recapped and reassessed discussion.

Dear friend Danny Postel is one of those people.

We met through my brother Jon 14 years ago in May, and instantly started riffing on books and justice and basketball and women.

We've been talking ever since.

In a lot of ways, and for a long time, Danny was an experience as much as a friend.

Alternately erudite and bawdy, contemplative and insatiably gregarious, brash and sensitive, he was easily one of the five largest personalities I had ever met.

Middle age, fatherhood and life's inevitable bumps, bruises and setbacks have tempered and toned him down somewhat, and his core remains quite firmly intact.

Regular readers of this space have read about Danny's inimitable capacity to bring people together–a skill and commitment that is so developed that I've extended the category of "connector" from Malcolm Gladwell's first book, *The Tipping Point*, to "uber-connector" to accurately depict Danny's behavior in this area.

He constantly shares articles and ideas and people and events and movements with those who come into his orbit.

It's not done in a scattershot or random way, either.

Danny has certain people with whom he links me for discussions about fatherhood, a different set for South Africa, a third group for things Latino, and so on.

And I'm just one of his many, many friends.

Although one of his most pronounced talents, Danny's capacity for connection is just one of the many distinctive aspects of his personality and life commitments.

He's an impressive, accomplished and exuberant athlete whose long-range shooting in basketball, powerful serves in tennis and outbursts of trash and self-talk are the stuff of legend.

He's a dedicated father who spends enormous amounts of time with his sons Elijah and Theo.

Danny's also a prolific, versatile and disciplined writer as well as a meticulous editor.

After stints as the host of Free Associations Radio and staff reporter at the Chronicle of Higher Education, Danny has written one book, *Reading Legitimation Crisis in Tehran: Iran and the Future of Liberalism*, and co-edited, with Nader Hashemi, a second work, *The People Reloaded: The Green Movement and the Struggle for Iran's Future*.

Both are testaments to his intellectual curiosity, his love of thoughtful argument, and his unusual capacity to assign, and then carry out, substantial projects that bring together his passions for philosophy, cultural diversity and social justice.

The first book grew out of an essay he wrote that explored the question of why the American Left, which had been so outraged during the 1980s about governmental mistreatment in El Salvador and other Central American nations, was almost completely silent about similar levels of abuse visited on Iranians.

His answer was that Iran did not fit into the same paradigm of being on the receiving end of American imperialism as the Central American countries with whom so many on the American Left had expressed such fervent solidarity.

That initial essay led to his securing a contract from the University of Chicago Press' *Prickly Paradigm Press* series to write a short book that included, among other things, an exploration of the rapturous reception Jürgen Habermas received in Iran compared with the comparatively total indifference in the United States and an extended interview with Ramin Jahanbegloo.

Again, Danny's propensity to bring together people with shared ideals and different cultural backgrounds and life experiences shines through the work. The book contains a series of essays of varying lengths from contributors as varied as Nobel Peace Prize winner Shirin Ebadi to former regular MacNeil/ Lehrer Report guest Gary Sick.

Here's what I wrote at the time:

"Generally brief, these interviews, essays, reflections, letters and thought pieces cover nearly every conceivable angle of the revolution's source, repression and state a year later. While the Ahmadinejad government did seem to succeed in putting down the uprising in the short term, the message of eventual victory is a consistent theme that resonates throughout the work.

In keeping with what I know of Danny, the book also delves into the complexities of the revolution, including a number of pieces about the role of women, the connection to the larger geopolitical scene in the Middle East, and the role Green Leader Mir Hossein Mousavi played in the murder of many Iranian citizens during the 80s. (To be fair, Mousavi gets pretty light and sympathetic treatment on this front.)"

Danny's collaboration with Nader on *The People Reloaded* will now have a promising afterlife: Danny is moving from Chicago to Denver to become the Associate Director of the Center for Middle East Studies at the University of Denver.

Nader is directing the new research center.

The other evening Danny and I got together at one of his favorite restaurants, Garden of Eden, right near the corner of California and Touhy.

In typical fashion, he greeted the owners and workers in Spanish, English and Assyrian, depending on their first language. (He speaks the first two fluently and has a smattering of words in the latter. He also has functional proficiency in Italian.)

We gathered to celebrate, mark the end of this stage, and note the beginning of his new adventure.

In some ways, it's hard to overstate how odd it will be not to have Danny in Chicago.

He's been here full time since he moved back from living in Washington, DC while working for the *Chronicle*, and has been enormously encouraging and inclusive of me as a journalist, father and friend.

When we started playing tennis together on a regular basis, Danny bought me a racket.

He invited me to Sunday night basketball games at the Robert Crown Center in Evanston.

He's sent me countless books and articles, and, in one of his most profoundly generous acts, commissioned me to write an extensive profile of MacArthur Award-winning psychologist, professor and author Robert Coles.

This was a tremendous vote of confidence and a true gift.

I had read Coles' work for years, but would not have created the opportunity to meet him had Danny not called me with the assignment.

I opened the piece by showing the reader what I had seen in Coles' Concord home:

"To understand Robert Coles' two latest books, it helps to have seen his writing chair.

Comfortable and unassuming, it sits with a blanket draped over it in the study of the three-story house in Concord, Massachusetts, where he and his late wife, Jane, raised their three boys.

The wall opposite the chair features a gallery of framed black-and-white photographs of his personal heroes, many of whom appear in his books—here is William Carlos Williams; there is Walker Percy; and there, in the bottom row, is a smiling Bruce Springsteen, his arm around Coles' shoulder, like a brother. The chair is where Coles has sat and written, on long sheets of yellow lined paper, dozens of books, including volumes of poetry, a novel, and books for children and adults, as well as thousands of scholarly articles and reviews.

It was in that chair that Coles wrote the books that made him a major public intellectual in the 1960s and 1970s, before the term was in use. Children of Crisis, a five-volume series, remains perhaps his most famous work. The series examines the moral and spiritual lives of children across the country with a poignancy that struck a deep chord in the culture. (In 1973 Coles received the Pulitzer Prize for Volumes Two and Three.)

During those years Coles also worked as a speechwriter for Robert Kennedy, crafting the senator's final speech before his assassination in 1968. But he by no means operated exclusively behind the scenes: his writings appeared in the pages of Harper's, The New Yorker, and The Atlantic Monthly; he could be seen on The Dick Cavett Show; and his name and reputation were familiar to a wide swath of Americans."

The fourth paragraph in particular bears Danny's imprint and insistence that I explain why the reader who did not already know Coles should care about him.

We had talked about, but not gotten together, to celebrate the March publication of the essay, so tonight's meal had several layers to it.

As always, the conversation flowed smoothly and effortlessly.

We jumped from fatherhood to the Chicago teachers strike to our new video project to the year in men's tennis to physical ailments to his new job, talking and listening to each other with equal gusto, patience and excitement.

After a couple of hours, we were ready to walk along the wet sidewalks with his bike.

We strolled along the couple of blocks to his beloved Indian Boundary Park–the park in which he has raised his sons and where we played tennis many times–sharing intimate stories of gratitude for all that we have received in our lives. Our appreciation is more, not less, heightened by the struggles we've confronted and endured.

Eventually, it was time for us to end the latest installment of our ongoing life conversation and head to our respective homes. Danny had a tennis tournament in the morning, while I had a Dart Society board meeting.

Before we left, we hugged and thanked each other for our shared friendship.

I got in our car to drive home, while Danny biked toward his place.

I don't know when Danny and I will see each other again.

But I do know what will happen when we do.

We'll smile.

We'll jump up and down and exchange high fives and hugs.

We'll sit down.

And then we'll talk.

PAT NAVIN'S COURAGEOUS FUNDRAISING BIKE RIDE

July 22, 2012

Friend and neighbor Pat Navin, center, with his treatment team.
Dr. Stanley Liauw is on right.
(Photo courtesy of Pat Navin)

Not even Lance Armstrong did this.

The seven-time Tour de France winner who is the subject of the latest in a seemingly unending series of doping allegations and lawsuits was, in happier times, known for his transformation from cancer survivor to cycling legend.

But friend and neighbor Pat Navin has done the Texan one better for the past seven weeks.

Every Monday through Friday since May 29, the lean and lanky Navin has donned his biking outfit in the early morning. He's mounted his trusty copper LeMond Wayzata, pedaled from his house on Cleveland Street in Evanston to the Lake Shore trailhead at the intersection of Ardmore and Sheridan roads and ridden along the spectacular route to the University of Chicago.

Once at his destination, he's been treated for an aggressive form of prostate cancer that he learned about last October.

At the beginning of the process, Pat said he didn't know if he would be able to ride every day. The side effects of his hormone therapy and radiation are numerous.

These include, but are not limited to, fatigue, nausea and "rectal urgency." Pat's had those.

On the third day, he encountered a torrential downpour and 49 degree temperatures.

The last couple of weeks have brought many days of blistering heat.

But he's kept riding.

Pat's been treated by a dedicated team headed by Dr. Stanley Liauw, a radiation oncologist, clinician and researcher.

After the daily treatment, Pat's biked to the Millennium Bike Center where he is a fixture, showered and changed. And he's put in work at the advertising agency he owns before getting on the bike and heading for home.

That's 44.7 miles per day.

By Monday, when he'll have his final day of treatment, Pat will have ridden nearly 1,800 miles. (This only adds to the nearly 40,000 miles he's put on the bike since buying it in 2002.) As he said wryly, "That's like riding from Chicago to Las Vegas without the dancing girls, Wayne Newton or Cirque du Soleil."

On one level, for people who know Pat, this routine is not surprising.

Those of us who frequent the bike shed know there are varying levels of commitment to riding.

Pat's is among the very top.

Regardless of the season or available light in the morning or evenings, he very rarely misses a day of commuting on his bike. His riding during his treatment, then, can be seen as an extension of an activity for which he has deep passion and in which he finds serenity, joy and meaning.

But let's be real here.

This is an extraordinary display of guts and resistance in the face of a relentless disease that has among its many consequences the erosion of one's physical being.

Pat's had company along the way.

He says that his wife Carol and friends Frank Shaw, Tom Waterloo, Tom Arndt and Steve Schwartz have allowed him to draft off them. (Although I know from having ridden with Pat, there's a strong chance they may be benefiting from his going first into the wind.)

A little while ago Pat also had an insight: he should use his riding as a fundraiser to help Liauw support his prostate research.

On Thursday he sent out a letter detailing his interrelated biking and cancer journeys and asking others to join him in this effort.

He wrote in part:

"Stan Liauw is an impressive person. He is intelligent, compassionate, honest and humble. When I told him that I would like to raise some money for his research (more on his research in a moment), he was welcoming, but quite humbled and grateful. He told me that even a couple thousand dollars would go a long way, allowing him to hire some graduate students to do, as he said, so much of the "grunt work" involved in clinical research.

So I am asking my friends and family members if they would do me a big favor and contribute to a fund dedicated to helping Stan's research projects. The fund is marked specifically for his work and not for the institution, at large, meaning you can rest assured that any donation you give will be going directly to the important work Stan is doing."

Dunreith and I are in, and I hope you'll be, too.

On Monday, about a dozen friends will gather at 6:30 a.m. at the Navin house to accompany him on the last of his 38 treatments. After completing the ride, they'll have some coffee and celebrate the end of this chapter.

Knowing Pat, it is likely to be a celebration animated by a visceral understanding of life's fragility.

Cancer is a brutal disease.

Sadly, the hard truth is none of us know what will happen to him.

But we do know what he's done and how he's faced one of the biggest, if not the biggest, challenge of his full life.

Until recently, and still for many, Lance Armstrong has been considered the standard of courage in the face of cancer.

I know who I've got.

He doesn't live in Austin, Texas.

MAKING HISTORY WITH VUKANI

Dec. 13, 2011

Celebrating with Fulbright brother Vukani Cele.
(Photo courtesy of Jeff Kelly Lowenstein)

"**W**e are making history again, Jeff!" Vukani exclaimed as we walked amongst a streaming mass of fanatical Orlando Pirates supporters on our way to the spanking new Moses Mabhida stadium.

I was inclined to agree.

Playing, coaching and watching soccer had been a major component of my participation in the Fulbright Teacher Exchange Program in South Africa during the 1995-1996 school year.

One of my most memorable experiences came early in the year, when Tsepo, one of Vukani's best friends, drove me to Johannesburg for the finals of the Four Nations Cup that pitted South Africa against Tunisia.

When Ntuthuko, another friend, realized that the number of tickets was one short of the number needed for all of us to go, he broke the news to me with a seriousness that I could only assume he had learned during the portion of his medical training that dealt with informing people they have little time left to live.

"You see, Jeff," he said. "The problem is that we don't have enough tickets. How would you feel about staying here while we watched the game?"

"Not after I came all the way from Durban!" I responded.

"OK, Jeff," Ntuthuko said. "Don't worry. We will organize."

He was good to his word and returned several hours later not only with the promised ticket, but with one that was in the Vodacom box that meant we had access to ample supplies of food and drink.

I learned later that Tsepo, he and some of the other guys had planned to drug my Coke if their quest had been unsuccessful. I would sleep through the game, at which point they would return and upbraid me for being so sleepy.

Fortunately, that was not necessary. We all saw a dramatic 2-0 victory by Bafana, Bafana, the Zulu name for the beloved national team.

Vukani drew on a college connection to get us seats in the Presidential Suite. This was handy because of the tasty food and free-flowing beer because it was raining quite.

Vukani had further marked the significance of the occasion by giving me his son's black winter hat with the Pirates logo. (I had done my part by donning the navy blue blazer I wore when Dunreith and I got married for the second time at Look Park.)

The hat attracted plenty of attention.

I had trouble walking more than 25 yards without a crazed Pirates fan flashing in front of me, arms crossed in an X at the wrist to resemble bones and yelling, "Amabakhabakha," the Zulu name for the team, and pointing to my hat.

Ntuthuko was supposed to join us, but had to tend to being the deputy for the beginning of his niece's lobola, or bride negotiation process.

In the initial meeting, members of the groom's party comes to the bride's house to state their intentions and start to build a relationship with the families that will merge through the marriage.

Because of Ntuthuko's absence, Vukani had to sell two surplus tickets.

Rather than scalp them for a profit, he sold them at face value to a man who looked as if the 100 Rands, the equivalent of about $12, was an awful lot, but there was no way he was not going to take his woman to that game.

Pre-game festivities consisted of downing a couple of beers with Owen, an energetic events planner for whom Vukani had been the main negotiator during his lobola process several years before.

We headed up to the stands, got the guards to open up the gates and entered the box.

It was perfect.

Rather than being enclosed and distant from the other fans, the box was just a hop away from the passageway where the fans walked toward their seats. (This created some problems as a series of non-box fans tried to join the section.)

Moses Mabhida is an open dome with a looming arch. The stadium holds about 50,000 people, each of whom has at least a decent view of the field. The bright lights illuminated the perfectly manicured grass onto which a steady stream of rain fell.

I would guess that about 100 of us were white, another example of the apartheid government's comprehensive reach.

In that era, rugby and cricket were white sports. Soccer was black.

The stadium was part of South Africa's effort to host a "carbon neutral" world cup. In this case, it meant tearing down the existing stadium and rebuilding it with the same materials.

Yet in an unfortunate twist that illustrated the apartheid era's enduring legacy in the country, the soccer authorities apparently did not communicate about the field dimensions with the rugby officials who run Kings Park Stadium, which is adjacent to Moses Mabhida.

As a result, rugby games are rarely played in the new venue.

But all of that was far removed from our minds when the game began.

It was a sloppy affair, but one in which the Pirates struck first, just minutes into the game.

The goal set off a frenzy of celebration from the crowd, which was filled with 90, if not 95, percent Pirates supporters.

Vukani was right with them, dancing, pumping his fist in the air and yelling with glee.

The Pirates had a golden chance to put the game away just minutes later, but they failed to convert and the score held at halftime.

Vukani and I agreed that this meant that the opposing Wits squad was dangerous.

Twenty minutes into the second half, they tied the score.

The potential tie forced Pirates to dig deep within themselves. They responded, scoring a second goal on a left-footed blast, followed by a delightful clinching goal in which they moved the ball down the left flank before placing it by the frustrated goalkeeper.

Each successive score set off ever more exuberant and joyful celebrations which continued long after the game ended. Dozens of fans stormed the field before being tackled by the security guards who got in a few swift quick kicks to the miscreants.

Vukani couldn't have been happier.

The game was an important one, as Pirates were seeking to become the first club to hold all five major titles in one season. Last year they won the treble, a first in local football since the formation of South Africa's Premier Soccer League in 1996.

We asked someone to take a picture of us.

We stood arm in arm, cheering and holding our beers.

It reminded me of one we took when we first met 16 years ago in Washington, DC, near a monument for South African veterans. There, we also placed arms around each other's shoulders before setting off for our respective adventures.

More than a decade and a half later, that moment of connection was captured again, this time on Vukani's soil, over our shared passion for sport. Now middle-aged fathers and husbands, we were ever so grateful to be together, to share the experience and, indeed, to again make history.

SOURCES OF JOY: GERMANY TRIP COMING TOGETHER

April 16, 2012

Edward Lowenstein and Norbert Mering shake hands at Mering's home
in Germany in May 2012.
(Photo by Jon Lowenstein/NOOR)

Sometimes you don't realize how heavily an issue is weighing on you until something causes the pressure to lift.

That happened to me this morning when I pressed the "Submit" button on the United Airlines tickets we were buying for Dunreith, Aidan and me to go to Dad's hometown in Germany in late May.

Receiving our confirmation number meant that one of the last major pieces in the proverbial puzzle has come into place.

All of a sudden, I felt lighter.

Much lighter.

We've been talking for years, decades really, about going back to Germany with Dad to see the community where his family lived for close to 150 years before he was sent on a train to England and safety through the Kindertransport program.

At times, we even got beyond the general discussion to talking about specific months and dates.

But, somehow, Dad wasn't quite willing to return.

In the past year or so, though, his attitude has changed.

I've written before about Gabriele Thimm, the German teacher who contacted me last fall. She had read an article I had written about a previous trip I had taken to pursue family roots in Essen.

She invited us to a memorial service she was holding with her students for the town's Jewish community.

Two of Dad's cousins had been students at the school.

Unlike Dad and Uncle Ralph, his older brother, they did not have the good fortune to have escaped Hitler's Nazi regime.

Like more than 1 million other children, they were killed.

Gabriele sought to educate the students about our cousins and other members of the Essen community who were murdered.

Although invited, we could not attend the ceremony. Instead we sent a statement and family pictures that were projected onto the home of Joseph Lowenstein, our patriarch and my namesake.

Gabriele and I have been planning our trip for months, figuring out which days will work and what we'll do during the time that we are there.

Last week, she sent news that she had met with Mr. and Mrs. G. A client of my great-grandfather's, Mr. G.'s father owned a print shop. He was the person to whom Papa Joseph entrusted our family Bible shortly before he was transported to his death at Auschwitz.

The elder Mr. G. held the Bible for years before returning it to family members.

When I visited him in 2004, the son had a notebook filled with 65 years worth of correspondence between our families.

The first page was from 1931 and contained the death notice for my great-grandmother, Papa Joseph's wife.

The elder Mr. G. had made the card.

The final page was holiday greetings from Dad's cousin Jan in 1996.

In between were generations of connection across a continent and through some of the greatest atrocities our planet has ever witnessed.

This included a letter from Mr. G. the father to my Uncle Ernie explaining what had happened during the war.

The notebook also held receipts from care packages our family had sent theirs after the war.

It had instructions from Grandpa Max, my father's father, about what Mr. G. should do to help our family receive the reparations to which the German government had determined we were entitled.

More than 100 pages long, the notebook was a treasure trove that unlocked the answers to questions I had had for many years about Dad's background, but had struggled to have him answer directly.

Sitting in a cafe at which our ancestors had eaten, the G.s and Gabriele met and talked about our upcoming visit.

Yesterday, Gabriele sent the invitation to the event she will hold at the Great Synagogue.

Entitled, "A Celebration of Life," the invitation is set against the backdrop of my great-grandfather's stately and angular yellow house.

It welcomes people in the community to learn about our family's history in the town, and, by extension, Essen's Jewish community.

The event will have music and a reception afterward, the invitation said.

The invitation reinforced the trip's imminent arrival.

Buying those tickets cemented it.

At this point in life I've been around long enough to know that positive results and realized dreams and deeply held desires do not automatically happen.

Far from it, in fact.

But pressing that "Submit" button moved us a lot closer to moving this particular vision of family knowledge and experience from our head and hearts and into the world.

Today, that was enough to make me feel relief that we're finally making this happen, grateful that the tickets were there, and eager for whatever lies ahead for all of us.

I don't know exactly what is going to happen, or how Dad or anyone is going to find the time.

But I do know that I'm thrilled that we'll be there together to find out.

Our plane flies from O'Hare to Frankfurt in less than six weeks.

SOURCES OF JOY: ARRIVING IN GERMANY

June 2, 2012

German teacher Gabriele Thimm, center, at the surprise birthday party for Edward Lowenstein.
(Photograph by Jon Lowenstein/NOOR)

Her full head of bushy black hair bouncing as she skipped along the Essen train platform, her daughter Gloria at her side, Gabriele Thimm extended her arms toward me.

We hugged.

It was an embrace eight months in the making.

I had first heard from Gabriele last September, when she reached out to me online after having read a story I wrote in 2004 about searching for family roots in Germany.

She explained that she was a middle school teacher and was planning to hold a memorial service for Essen's Jewish community.

One of the houses at which they would be stopping during the memorial ceremony was Alte Zeilen 22, a tall and stately three-story yellow building that served as home and office for Joseph Lowenstein, my great-grandfather, namesake and a family doctor.

After being moved to a pre-deportation house in Steele, Joseph was deported to Theresienstadt in Czechoslovakia.

From there, he was taken to Izbica and the east, where he was killed in one of Poland's six death camps.

Gabriele had invited us to attend the ceremony.

With only six weeks notice, we had been unable to pull everyone together to go.

But we did send family pictures of my great-grandfather, of Aidan and Dunreith and of Mike's wedding in San Francisco.

We also sent the following statement:

Dear Ms. Thimm, parents, teachers, and members of the Essen-Steele community,

It is with gratitude and respect that we write this note to register our appreciation of the commitment you have shown to confront the dark chapter in Germany's past and to commemorate the lives of residents in the community who were killed during the Nazi era.

Ms. Thimm, we honor the courage, character and persistence you have shown in undertaking this project. We also want to acknowledge the support you have received from your supervisors and the other members of the community in making a public and permanent acknowledgment through these memorials of what happened here during the period when Adolf Hitler ruled the country.

This memorial and the ongoing teaching of the children about what occurred represents an important act of acknowledgment that has, in its process and substance, contributed to a healing process. It is also a critical, but not sufficient, element in allowing young people to emerge into adulthood with a full understanding of what has been part of their nation's past, but what need not be again should they act with the same decency and humanity demonstrated by so many of the people who are gathered here today.

We regret that we are not able to join you on this momentous occasion, but want to be emphatically clear that our inability to attend in person does not in any way signal a lack of awareness, appreciation and respect for what you have done and what you will continue to do this in this area.

We look forward to the day, hopefully this spring, when we will be able to meet and express our gratitude to you in person. In the meantime, we hope the ceremony goes well today. Please know that it is deeply appreciated by us.

Sincerely,

The Lowenstein Family

Gabriele sent us pictures from the event.

I spoke with our family members in December. Together we decided that this was the year we would finally take the trip we had discussed and planned for so many years.

Over the following weeks and months Gabriele and I forged plans for the week through emails and Skype.

I sent everyone on our side the updates, minus the plans to hold a surprise birthday party for Dad, who would be turning 78 the week that we were there.

The days sprinted into weeks. At the end of a grueling May, I found myself on a Thursday night packing for our adventure.

The flight went smoothly–heavy on *Godfather* films, light on sleep–we breezed through customs and waited a couple of hours for the train to take us to Essen, Dad's hometown. We boarded it and transferred in Cologne, sleeping for most of the two-hour journey.

Then we saw Gabriele and Gloria, an 18-year-old with an easy laugh, animated spirit and impeccable English.

They drove us to their house, where they had prepared a breakfast that was a three-hour lunch. Sitting in a beautifully peaceful enclosed garden that Gabriele and Gloria tend with care, we ate on plates with red hearts.

The spread was tremendous.

Exquisitely creamy cheese. Brotchen, or little pieces or bread. Nutella. Turkey salami. Hard-boiled eggs.

We sat and chatted and began the process of getting to know each other in person after having communicated for much of the past eight months about the trip's logistics.

I had known about her tremendous commitment to students' learning about Germany's past–"The next generation needs to know," she said, simply–but today got a better sense of her personal stake in the issue.

She explained that when she was about 5 years old, around Easter, her father came home with some Matzo and told her the story of Passover.

Her father had relatives named David and Rebekah, names that could have been Jewish, she said. But when she asked her parents about it, she was met with a stony silence.

In other words, Gabriele, like me, had a hunger to know about her family's history.

In the early 70s, she started wearing a Magen David, or Star of David, around her neck.

She's been wearing it since.

After a couple of hours, Gawain, Gabriele's 20-year old son, emerged after having stayed up all night at a friend's birthday party. Sporting sunglasses, a leonine head of thick brown hair and a goatee, he explained that while one should not have a beer before 4:00 p.m., he was not violating that edict because it was after 4:00 p.m. yesterday.

We all chuckled appreciatively.

Dunreith, Aidan and I started to fade as the food started to settle in our stomachs and combine with the jet lag to make our eyelids shut themselves.

Gabriele drove us back to the hotel where we staying.

We collapsed for about three hours, connected with Jon, who had arrived after us, and had some Spargel, or white asparagus, at Pfefferkorn, a restaurant that served typical German fare.

I had had some success dusting off my rusty German-speaking skills, which now had serious recall competition from Spanish since I work at *Hoy*, the Chicago Tribune Company's Spanish-language newspaper.

But I did make a mistake with Gabriele, erroneously thinking that "halb neun" meant 9:30, not 8:30.

This only meant that our indefatigable host tracked us down at the restaurant where we had agreed to meet. Her children and Jan, Gloria's boyfriend, a blond, blue-eyed young man with glasses and a passion for music festivals, accompanied her.

We all drank and sat and chatted some more before heading to the train station to meet Dad and his partner, Lee Kass.

He would soon be setting foot in his hometown for the first time in 73 years.

DAD AND LEE ARRIVE IN GERMANY

June 4, 2012

Three generations of Lowensteins gather in Essen with German teacher
Gabriele Thimm in May 2012.
(Photograph by Jon Lowenstein/NOOR)

"**I** think that's your Dad's head," Dunreith said as we climbed up the stairs to the train in Gate 4 at Essen's Hauptbahnhof station.

As is often the case with my wife, she was right.

We made it up the remaining few steps. I had to call Dad's name a few times before he heard me and turned around to greet us.

It was happening.

We were all together in Essen.

The last time Dad had set foot in this part of the country was more than 73 years earlier.

He had left on a train with a number around his neck signifying his participation on the Kindertransport, a program the British government created in the aftermath of the Kristallnacht rampage that saw Jewish homes, businesses, synagogues and lives destroyed and burned to the ground on November 9 and 10, 1938.

During our childhood, Dad would tell my brothers Mike, Jon and me that he remembered almost nothing from his close to five years in Germany. But one of the things he did remember was the Gestapo coming after Kristallnacht for his father Max.

His father was taken for weeks and returned bruised and badly beaten. Dad always wondered if the physical abuse our grandfather had endured contributed to his later deafness.

As a child, Mom told me how my grandmother Hilde had forced herself to dress up and put on lipstick to appeal to the police to release her husband.

The pogrom and his subsequent incarceration convinced Grandpa Max, a disabled World War I veteran who lost at least part of his hearing in that conflict, that the Hitler government would never come to its senses and stop the ceaseless advances to eliminate Jews from German civic life.

Hilde had a cousin in England who helped find a place for Dad and Ralph, his elder brother, in the country near Southampton, about an hour south of London.

Ralph left first.

The departure had not been easy.

Dad learned decades later that his father could not bring himself to leave the train that held his eldest son when he was supposed to do so at the first stop.

Instead he spoke to the train officials and got permission to get off after the next one.

But he couldn't do it there, either.

This went on for several stops, only ending when my grandfather was forcibly thrown from the train.

After recovering from an emergency appendectomy, Dad followed a couple of weeks later.

He and Ralph lived for close to 18 months with Ruth Stern, a university-educated classics scholar and primary school principal. An eccentric British Jew, she retired near the Golan Heights in Israel, "the land of the Bible."

She treated the boys with utmost consideration and kindness. Dad remembered spending nights in the house's bomb shelter during the early stages of the Battle of Britain as a great adventure.

So when he and Ralph departed for the United States in late 1940, it was the second such emotional rupture in their young lives.

After reuniting with their parents in New York, Dad and Ralph moved with them to Cincinnati. There, Max and Hilde set up the task of rebuilding a life in a country where they knew few people, spoke little English and had no profession that could transfer from Germany, where my grandfather had been a lawyer.

They formed a community with other German Jewish refugees. Grandpa Max shifted from being a lawyer to an accountant. Through dint of will and grit and hard work, they made their way in the new and unexpected country of residence.

They didn't look back.

They definitely didn't talk about what they had experienced.

And they never returned to their homeland.

When we were young, Dad also didn't talk about what he had been through.

As a seventh grader, I remember watching the first installation of the mini-series *Holocaust*.

Dad stiffened and shut the television off, but insisted that nothing was wrong when we asked him.

He also did not go back to Duisburg, the community next to Essen where he was born.

This was not because he lacked opportunity to do so.

In 1965, with my pregnant mother in tow, and me in utero, Dad rode a train that stopped in Duisburg.

But, in a different way than his father a generation earlier, he was not ready to get off.

So he didn't.

This time, though, along with his life partner, Lee Kass, Dad stepped off the train and into a fuller confrontation with his past.

Looking cheerful and relaxed after two weeks in Paris and Normandy, he smiled and greeted Gabriele Thimm, the remarkable German teacher who had reached out to me and helped organize our visit, and her family as we rejoined them in the VaBene café a short walk from the station.

We got some drinks and coffee and desserts and sat around two long wooden tables outside the café. The Germans and Dunreith on one side, the three generations of Lowensteins and Lee on the other. We talked about the German school system and the cost of education in our respective countries and our thoughts about the prospects for Obama's re-election.

The sky was marvelously clear. After we finished, we walked by the old Lichtburg Theater in town, which Gabriele said used to have a Jewish owner.

She also told us about Ernest Blom, a Jew in Essen who helped feed hundreds of people each day before being taken away and killed by the Nazi government. The man who took over his store continued to send money to Blom's children, she said.

We saw the bustle of Muslim and Turkish and black African and Chinese workers and all gathered in a circle near the hotel.

"It's unbelievable you're all here," Gabriele said.

Like my wife just a couple of hours earlier, she was right.

Our adventure had begun.

VISITING THE JEWISH CEMETERY IN ESSEN

June 8, 2012

Edward Lowenstein pushes a branch aside at the Jewish cemetery in Essen
where generations of his ancestors are buried.
(Photograph by Jon Lowenstein/NOOR)

Dr. Uri Kaufmann led us from the street down the walking path, dug in his
pocket and found the key to Essen's Jewish cemetery.

He turned the lock and opened the door.

We entered a space that looked like an enchanted forest with air that
smelled like redwoods. Shards of light shimmered through the pine and other
trees that enveloped the space like a cocoon.

About 200 graves stood in six rows. The place had a hint not so much of disrepair, but of natural overgrowth. Many of the graves had moss on them, with plants like ferns and rhododendrons growing around them.

A German shepherd loomed in the distance above the tallest wall.

About 6 feet tall, with clear blue eyes, Kaufmann wore a light blue shirt and black shoes and had ridden his bicycle to the cemetery. Recently appointed to his post as director of the former Old Synagogue in Essen, which is now a cultural center, he often turned his wrist to check his watch.

He started the tour.

The cemetery opened in the mid-19th century, he said. Christians designed each of the graves because Jews were not allowed in that guild of workers. Their influence was notable in the stone urns that were atop some of the graves. Most were in German, with a few in Hebrew.

I had seen the cemetery with Mr. and Mrs. G. in 2004.

Indeed, the death notice of my great-grandmother Clara printed by Mr. G's father was the first page in a notebook in which the couple had compiled more than 65 years of correspondence between our two families.

But I hadn't been able to enter.

Kaufmann informed us that he did his doctoral work on Jewish and Christian cattlemen in the 19th century before telling us that our ancestors were probably cattle herders.

I had always heard we came from a famous line of rabbis, I answered, before remembering that was Mom's side, not Dad's.

Perhaps it was both, he replied crisply.

Although I had known about Clara being there in her final resting place, I didn't realize we had other relatives in the cemetery.

Four of them, in fact.

Their burial sites illustrated the changing fortunes of the Jewish community in the town and country as a whole.

Moses and Amalie, who we later learned owned a large farm called Hemmerhof in a more rural part of the city and who died in the early part of the 20th century, had the largest grave. Covered with a canopy of rhododendron, it was shaped like an obelisk. Dr. Kaufmann looked on in dismay as Jon and I pushed through the plants to photograph and take notes.

Clara, who died in 1931, shortly before the Nazis came to power, had a smaller burial site with a dark headstone that somehow had had the inscription removed.

And Fanny Lowenstein, a cousin who died in 1940, just had a stone in the ground.

A half-dozen soccer balls kicked over the wall by children sat like oversized Easter eggs, a reminder of the world outside the enclave.

For all the growth of greenery, the graves looked remarkably intact, I commented to Hoffman.

They were preserved, he said, because even during the Nazi era, people in the surrounding area retained a basic religious sense that kept them from desecrating graves.

Lee said the German shepherd, an animal the Nazis transformed from an animal herder to a vicious symbol of racial purity, was watching over us.

Kaufmann checked his watch again.

We thanked him.

He nodded and said he would see us at the ceremony the next day before getting back on his bike and pedaling away as if he were late for an appointment.

I stood there for a minute with my family in the late morning sun, wondering what happens when we add layers of knowledge and understanding to a past that was previously blank, when we go to a sacred place of permanent rest that, though overgrown, somehow survived the most horrific of genocidal regimes and is still here.

I didn't know the answers.

But I did know that I was grateful to have the chance to find out.

We piled into our white Nissan mini-van and drove back to the hotel.

CEREMONY OF LIFE AT THE OLD SYNAGOGUE IN ESSEN

June 29, 2012

Members of the Essen community gather for a Ceremony of Life
at the Old Synagogue that is now a cultural center.
(Photograph courtesy of Gabriele Thimm)

Everything came together today at the Old Synagogue.

The high-domed building with a purple cupola and orange walls is no longer a functioning religious site, but rather a cultural and educational institution.

It's headed by Dr. Uri Kaufmann, who showed us the cemetery. He smiled appreciatively as we arrived at 10:30. "Punctlich," he said. "Very good."

Kaufmann gave us a tour of the building, which had windows and mosaics destroyed in Kristallnacht and it sustained further damage in the 1960s, when people wanting to make a museum of industrial design removed the Torah ark. The ark was repaired in the mid-80s, but the Torah was never replaced as a reminder of that displacement.

Hundred of students, a dozen of whom had prepared for months for this day, were waiting there.

So were the rest of the people we had met during the week.

We sat in the seats assigned to us in the front row, donned red headsets and prepared to listen to the translation.

Kaufmann and the town's deputy mayor made introductory comments stressing the importance of the day.

The Ceremony of Life that Gabriele Thimm designed began with a family picture from the 1920s.

Papa Joseph was there with his four boys–Max, Rudi, Albert and Ernie. So, too, were my great-grandmother Clara and Rudi's wife, Margarete. The men all wore suits.

They were a typical-looking German family.

A young woman named Stephanie read first.

"For months we have been looking forward to say hello to you here today," she said in a firm tone. "Thank you for coming and welcome to Essen."

The program put the picture in the context of the family's history, talking about our ancestors Abraham and Moses Lowenstein and showing their arrival in Steele through documents and pictures.

The text went back into the past of the Jewish people up to the destruction of the Jewish temple, moved to the Jews in Germany and Essen, and then back again to our family.

A student named Melina explained why she and other students had participated in the ceremony.

"This is neither because we feel like offenders nor because we feel like victims, but because it is our concern to remember those people who lived in Essen as respected citizens, as friends, as acquaintances, as sport comrades, as parents, as employers and employees, in fact as citizens of the city of Essen," she read.

The students took us through the rise of the Nazi Party, the Kristallnacht pogrom, the creation of the Kindertransport program on which Dad and Uncle Ralph escaped, and Dad's departure from the country.

A pair of girls sang songs like "Hallelujah" by Leonard Cohen and "I Hope You Don't Mind" by Elton John at intervals throughout the ceremony.

At the end, the floor was opened to the students. They took a while to gather their nerve, but then their questions started coming.

What was it like in England?

What was the role of the women?

What do you think about Germany now?

Why are you here and why did you take this trip?

Dad stood up and began to speak.

He looked a little tight at first, but started relaxing and even told a couple of jokes through a story about mistaking the word "kitchen" for "prison" that elicited a chuckle from the crowd. (The words are very similar in German.)

Speaking in slow, clear tones, he told about how Grandpa Max refused to get off the train with Uncle Ralph until the authorities threw him off it.

He spoke about Ruth Stern's firm kindness and about how well he was treated in England.

He said some of the worst things that people have ever done to each other had happened in Germany.

But he also said the country has done more to reckon with its past than any country of which he was aware in history.

Dad also read a statement that announced the creation of a Lowenstein Award to honor young people who, through their writing or actions, embody values of tolerance and acceptance of people from all backgrounds.

Standing in the same area where our forebears had been before the laws and the exile and the murders, I felt linked as never before to history and the future and confrontation and reconciliation.

I spoke in German about how being there was a dream coming true for us as a family. I talked about the gifts they gave us through their presence and complimented the young people who had done so well during the ceremony.

I also said that we understood that it is not easy to be a young person, but we are here for them, we believe in them and we know that they can learn from history, not just the bad parts, but from people like the gentleman who had helped our family.

Together we can build a better world, I said.

We were brought forward to the podium, where Gabriele read the following:

May I ask you to join me once more. I want to reveal to everybody here that Dr. Löwenstein celebrated his birthday yesterday, on 29th May. He was 5 years old when he had to leave Essen to survive, and now, after 73 years, he is back for the first time. Almost everything has changed–and fortunately, many things have improved.

But even today, we don´t live in a land of milk and honey.

We still have to create our own paradise.

Knowing history and remembering is the only way to make sure people can work on future freedom, security and peace. While antisemitism increases and there are frequent menaces to extinguish Israel, we still won´t give up hope that young people will learn to think on their own and withstand indoctrination and manipulation to live a life in freedom.

We would like to give you a symbol for paradise–honey. It´s honey from the hills alongside the river Ruhr. The beekeeper is a former colleague who has retired–Norbert Mering.

Gabriele gave Dad a big bottle of honey from Norbert for his birthday and all the rest of us smaller containers of the sweet nectar.

We all sang Happy Birthday to Dad.

Then it was over.

We ate the food that had been prepared for us, shook hands and talked with the dozens of students and adults who had attended and wanted to connect.

At moments I felt mobbed, but mostly I felt grateful for what we had been privileged to experience.

It was a knowledge and public honoring of our family beyond anything we had ever known before, the beginning of what I'm confident will be an ongoing relationship, and an example of the possibility of reconciliation and healing that will lead to unknown destinations.

For the moment, though, the fact of the ceremony was more than beautiful enough.

We all walked back to the hotel to collapse and then face the rest of the day.

CEREMONY OF LIFE
AT REALSCHULE UBERRUHR

July 2, 2012

Edward Lowenstein shakes hands with a student at the Realschule Uberruhr
after the second Ceremony of Life.
(Photograph by Jon Lowenstein/NOOR)

"Herzlich Willkommen Familie Lowenstein," the sign with multi-colored individual letters exclaimed as we entered the middle school gym at the Realschule Uberruhr.

This was the second day we were to have a Ceremony of Life, designed and carried out by the intrepid and indefatigable Gabriele Thimm.

But if yesterday's event was cloaked in ceremony and pomp and greetings from luminaries, today's was pure middle school.

You could see it in the basketball hoop in front of the sign, in the wiggling and occasional smiles of the students as the program moved forward, and in their fresh and innocent faces as they came forward to place brown roots or light green leaves on the dark green Stammbaum, or family tree, Gabriele had created. In all, it would show seven generations of Lowensteins, culminating in our son Aidan as the most recent descendent of the line.

The tree was one of many ways Gabriele tweaked the program to make it more interactive for the students.

She regularly inserted questions for the tenth grade students to ask the younger ones and to comment on their responses. She put in a surprise version of Hava Nagila in which the students danced round and round, then came over to us in the front row and pulled us into the circle. The group turned into a line that snaked around the entire gym.

The other addition to this second Ceremony of Life was about Dad.

After talking with Jon and Dunreith, I had mentioned to Gabriele that yesterday's program had not talked much about Dad's life after the war, about how he had absorbed this traumatic and devastating experience and embraced the educational and career opportunities afforded him. He would make his mark on the world as a doctor, professor, teacher and mentor who became known as the father of cardiac anesthesia.

He did so without forgetting where he had come from, all the while reaching out to refugees, sticking up for people who had suffered injustice, and continuing the tradition of accomplishment and excellence he had inherited before the family tree had been ruptured.

To her credit, Gabriele inserted the information into the meat of the second program.

As opposed to the more formal program yesterday, when the request for questions for Dad took a long time to generate a response, today they came easily and freely.

"Did you ever see your parents again?"

"Does your family like soccer?"

"What do you think of Germany today?"

"What was it like when you saw your parents again?"

Dad answered in his halting but ever improving German, switching to English and then back to talking slowly again in his native tongue.

The students' questions came from all over the room. While they were cut off after 15 minutes, they clearly could have gone for much, much longer.

The school wished Dad a collective Happy Birthday and us a safe trip home.

The ceremony was over and we had to run to catch the train, but not before a line of kids approached Dad to shake his hand and ask him some more questions and before we all took pictures near the Stammbaum.

Just as they had when we arrived, Gabriele and Gloria dropped us at the station.

The train was a quarter hour late, so we sat around and talked about how much we had done and what we would do after we all recovered from our fatigue.

Gabriele looked at once radiant and exhausted in her fire-red shoes and lipstick.

It seemed almost impossible to believe that just eight months ago we had never written or spoken to each other.

The train came on the other track. The door closed on Lee as she tried to enter it, so we had to sprint and chuck our bags from the platform onto the train lobby.

This made our hugs with Gabriele and Gloria more rushed, but no less heartfelt.

Seventy-three years ago, Dad had boarded a train from the nearby town.

His departure into exile to save his life caused a wound that is still healing and occurred during a time when damage happened that can never be undone.

But this time, he came as a free man toward the end of a highly contributory and accomplished life, with large chunks of his family and a woman he had first known as a young man.

This time he was honored and celebrated and treasured beyond anything we had imagined.

Our visit did not, could not, undo what had happened.

But perhaps it provided some measure of healing and a weaving of new possibilities for Dad, for our family and for the town where he once lived and to which he had so many years later returned.

"CARRY OUT THEIR EMIGRATION": FOUR WORDS THAT REVEAL A UNIVERSE

Dec. 24, 2012

Edward Lowenstein looks at documents at 22 Alte Zeilen,
the home where his grandfather Joseph Lowenstein lived.
(Photograph courtesy of Jon Lowenstein/NOOR)

Sometimes four words can reveal a universe.

In this case, they were written at the end of a treasured gift given to us by Dirk Fuchs, who resides with his wife and younger son reside on the first floor at 22 Alte Zeilen in the Steele neighborhood of Essen.

The home used to belong to Joseph Lowenstein, my great-grandfather and namesake.

Like Jews throughout the country, Papa Joseph endured the gradually and incessantly constricting clutches of the Nazi regime that stripped him of the medical license he had worked so hard to earn. Instead, he was called a "medical practitioner."

For a while, he was allowed to operate only on Jewish patients.

Later in the 1930s, he was not permitted to practice at all.

Joseph's son Ernie was also a doctor. Family legend has it that Joseph's four sons had a remarkably brief career-decision process. Their father pointed to two of them and told them they would be lawyers. The other two would be doctors.

This is precisely what happened.

"One didn't disobey one's parents," Ernie told me a half-century later while living in a retirement facility in Evansville, Indiana.

Ernie, who was in his mid-20s and did not have a family, responded by leaving his homeland, serving in the United States Army and working for close to 50 years as a country doctor in Mt. Carmel, Illinois.

Papa Joseph, however, decided to stay.

He did so because he was older.

He did so because he had known no other country and believed that Germany was his land.

He did so because, as the Lowenstein patriarch, he felt duty-bound not to leave as long as there was another family member in the country.

Of course, this sense of obligation had its own snaring effect, as the next generation also would not depart as long as their parents were alive.

I remember years later visiting my great aunt Ilse at her apartment in Queens, New York. A highly intelligent woman who studied with Karl Jaspers and earned her PhD. from the University of Heidelberg in 1931, Ilse told me she knew she had to leave Germany in 1929. That was the year when one of her professors discovered that he was one-quarter Jewish and killed himself in the town square.

But she didn't depart until eight years later, after her husband Eric, my grandmother's brother, had buried his parents.

Had they waited even one year longer, I might never have been conceived.

For it was Ilse who signed the affidavit that first permitted my grandparents, and then my father, to have an entry point in the United States.

For his part, Joseph stayed despite the persistent entreaties of Mr. G., a patient, Gentile and friend.

The owner of a print shop, Mr. G. wrote the death card marking the passing of my great-grandmother Clara in 1931. He saw the ominous and lethal direction in which the country was headed and implored his former physician to leave.

Joseph refused.

Unable to make a living, his financial situation worsened, we can only assume.

So in 1939, he decided to sell the three-story yellow home in which he had lived and worked.

His son Rudolf, also a doctor, had moved into the home with his family because he too could not make a living.

This brings us to Mr. Fuchs, who now lives in the home.

A civil servant, he spent a month in which he went through three city departments, calling in favors all along the way, to procure a copy of the bill of sale.

The dining room table on the first floor of Joseph Lowenstein's former home in Essen, Germany. Edward Lowenstein had had his appendix removed on the kitchen table in the same floor the last time he had been in the house more than 73 years earlier. *(Photo courtesy of Jon Lowenstein/NOOR)*

He presented the document to us on May 29, 2012.

He gave it to us at the kitchen table, which was filled with plates, teacups, saucers and an exquisite array of homemade cakes and pastries baked with inordinate care and tenderness by his wife, Susan.

It was Dad's 78th birthday and the first time he had been in the house in 73 years.

The last time had been under far less hospitable conditions.

He was having his appendix removed on Papa Joseph's kitchen table.

His father Max, a World War I veteran, had taken his ailing son from doctor to doctor throughout the town where our family had lived for close to 150 years.

None would operate on a Jewish child.

This time, though, could not have been more different.

In addition to giving Dad the bill of sale, Dirk also gave the building's original floor plans and a piece of plaster that Susan had discovered while they were doing some work on the bathroom. She said she had to save it for Dad.

Edward Lowenstein looks at documents about his family presented to him by the owner of the first floor of his grandfather's former home in Essen, Germany.
(Photo courtesy of Jon Lowenstein/NOOR)

Like so many documents from the Hitler regime, the bill of sale looks ordinary enough.

It details the date of sale and the recipients of the 3,000 Deutschmarks a half-dozen members of our family received after the war in reparations to terminate our claim on the building.

It also identifies the buyer, a butcher in town, and the price of 19,000 Deutschmarks he paid for the stately building that was largely covered with ivy when we saw it.

But a curious phrase is embedded in the document, after the price and before the reparations. It says that Papa Joseph, Rudi and his family can stay in the house until they "carry out their emigration."

At first glance, the clause seems to be a generous gesture of a purchase by an area merchant to a well-liked, yet increasingly marginalized community member.

But a deeper look uncovers other aspects of the document and its contents.

The first is the assumption of an emigration.

This is curious on a number of levels. The most basic is that for much of the Nazi reign during which they lived, neither Papa Joseph nor Rudi wanted to leave the country.

In 2004 I learned that Papa Joseph eventually heeded his friend's advice and sought to leave.

He walked around the town of Essen with an English dictionary seeking to gain proficiency in the language he would need to speak when he landed in the United States, the country where his oldest son had been able to settle.

Joseph never made it.

Rudi also changed his mind and tried to depart from Germany.

But it was too late for him and his family as well.

Beyond our family members' individual desires, the ability of any Jews to emigrate at the dawn of the Second World War was severely limited-a fact which makes the verb "carry out" more than a little curious.

While it is true that my father's parents, escaped through Genoa, Italy in 1940, they were rare exceptions to an increasingly restrictive policy.

Another point: The purchase took place after the so-called period of Aryanization began.

The late Holocaust scholar David Bankier once talked about the circles of involvement within German society in regards to the Nazi Party.

Just 10 percent of the population belonged to the Party, he said.

But many other people who were not Nazis supported it by participating in the Aryanization of the country.

This happened in 1938.

It consisted of German non-Jews purchasing businesses and homes from Jews at the dirt cheap prices with little room for dissent from the sellers.

Seen in this context, the purchase appears far from a magnanimous gesture, but rather to be another step in the degradation and later destruction of Papa Joseph and our family in particular, and the Jewish people in general.

This idea gains currency when one considers that the part of the phrase that said our family could remain in the house until they carried out their emigration did not turn out to be true.

Joseph was later forced to move from his home to a house where many Jews were placed before being deported and killed.

Joseph understood the fate that awaited him.

In an effort to preserve whatever precious family materials he could, he turned to Mr. G., the former patient who had pleaded with my great-grandfather to leave when could.

Shortly before his deportation, Joseph visited his former patient and friend, the Jewish family Bible in tow.

He had received the Bible, which contained vivid illustrations by Gustav Doré, to mark the occasion of his and Clara's 25th wedding anniversary.

On the front page, written in careful German script, was our family tree stretching back through the 20th and 19th centuries before settling in the late 18th century, when the Lowensteins first arrived in Steele.

He also asked Mr. G. to hold about two dozen literary classics, works by authors like Shakespeare and Goethe.

The man consented.

Shortly thereafter, my great-grandfather was forced to board a train "headed for the East."

We don't know where he died–I looked once in the archives at Yad Vashem and it only said, "Izbica," a Polish town–and have heard everything from Theresienstadt to Treblinka to Auschwitz from family members over the years.

Even more important, perhaps, than the precise location where the genocidal regime ended Papa Joseph's life, is the coded meaning within four simple words: "Carry out their emigration."

Taken by law-abiding citizens and under the guise of a transaction between equals, the purchase of the house at Alte Zeilen did not lead directly to Papa Joseph's killing.

But it was an important part of that process.

We did not have the opportunity to meet the butcher's descendants to hear their side of the story.

But the honor and decency with which Mr. G. acted means that other Germans like him had a choice, that their actions were not inevitable, and thus some judgment of what happened is possible.

Mr. G.'s actions raise a painfully tantalizing question: how might history have turned out if more Germans had had the moral compass and willingness to act as he did, rather than the anonymous butcher who bought our family's house?

We will never know, of course.

But we can take from that unrealized possibility a reminder not only to take moral actions ourselves, but also to work ceaselessly with others to ensure the social fabric and consensus is to protect, rather than prey on, our most vulnerable members.

That can take few words, too.

AGNES CONSADORI'S BOOK PARTY A BLAST

Dec. 10, 2010

It's a little after noon now, and I'm still glowing after last night's book party for *A Rainbow Of Memories: My Family's Journey From Piacenza to the United States.*

Held at Italian restaurant Pinstripes, the evening was filled with food, family and festivity.

Agnes of course was there, looking terrific, oozing satisfaction at having completed the project and gratitude to still be alive and vital at age 92.

A major portion of her family was there, too. This included heavy doses of the New Jersey and New York relatives about whom I had heard so much during the six years we had worked on the story of Agnes' family history.

Her daughter Lori, who had been the engine of the project, read a letter she had found that a relative had written to Agnes on her 80th birthday urging her to record and share all that she remembered.

And I gave the following toast:

"Agnes, Lori and I met for the first time in the summer of 2004. Agnes explained to me during our initial meeting that she had been telling some family stories after the funeral in January 2004 for Mary, who had been her last remaining sibling.

'Aunt Agnes, you remember so much about the family, you should write a book,' a niece said.

So she did.

Fortunately for me, I was hired to help make that happen.

Lori asked me when I thought we could finish the project.

I answered that it would definitely be done by Christmas.

Now, I will be honest and say that I thought we were talking Christmas 2004, not Christmas 2010.

Just to give a little bit of context, at the time we started the project the Boston Red Sox had not won a World Series since 1918, the year of Agnes' birth.

Barack Obama had gained national attention during a speech during the Democratic National Convention in which he called himself a "skinny kid with a funny name."

And a young grandson by the name of Marius Joseph Anthony Lucchetti was preparing to start first grade.

In those days, I was working for a small weekly community newspaper on Chicago's South Side. I'd finish my articles for the paper Thursday night, and then, every Friday, would drive out to Arlington Heights to meet with Agnes and Lori and hear the family stories.

Three things became immediately apparent to me.

First, Agnes is a fantastic storyteller. This led us to shift quickly from our initial plan of her telling me stories and my writing the family history from a third-person perspective to the book being in her voice.

Second, Agnes is a tremendously warm and generous person to whom family has meant everything.

And, third, she has an absolutely incredible memory.

In our conversations after the sessions, Lori and I would continually marvel at the volume and detail of the stories Agnes would recount. I mean, we are talking about Agnes remembering events to the day that happened when she was 2 years old, which at this point is a full 90 years ago. We would check, too!

Through the stories I had the privilege to get to know her family and to learn about their classically American journey from Piacenza and Ponte dell'Olio, Italy to America. I got to know Agnes' parents, Louis and Clara Losi, who set off for a new world, met, became engaged on their first date and built a loving home for their family. I got to picture Uncle Leo jumping off the Hellgate Bridge and Aunt Mary's elegance, to learn about the devoted love her brother John and his wife Gloria shared, to hear how her sister Louisa became Eloise the Fifth Avenue designer, to take pleasure in Aunt Claire's earning her college degree, and to imagine Agnes and Joe's courtship.

The family members became alive to me and a part of me.

Obviously, a lot has happened since we started.

The Red Sox have won two World Series.

Barack Obama is now completing the second year of his presidency.

And Marius recently began middle school.

A lot has happened in the family.

Bob has had and recovered from a heart attack.

Bob and Lori have torn down their house and built a new one where Agnes now lives.

Sadly, Aunt Claire has passed. I know she would have loved to be here, and somehow feel that she knows about today's celebration, is smiling and is willing to share her opinions.

Something else has happened, too.

The book.

Thanks to the collaboration between Agnes, Lori and my friend and colleague Christine Wachter, *A Rainbow of Memories* is a beautifully designed work full of stories and maps and letters and timelines and photographs, many of which you here sent to be included.

The book captures the full range of human emotions, from elation and tender connection to devastating sadness and loss.

Above all, it is based in Agnes' love for family and her desire to give to everyone in it.

In the book's Epilogue, Agnes writes the following:

I learned what was important in life from my parents. My mother and father worked hard, did not complain and appreciated what they earned. My mother would be in the kitchen every afternoon getting dinner ready for 6 p.m., when my father would come home from working as a tile setter. Our dinners were always full of tasty food, laughter and pleasure in being with each other.

My parents weren't wealthy, but they shared what they had with the family and they lived rich. My mother always had a nice cloth on the table and my father took great care in the wine he made and in his garden. My parents believed in taking pride in what you had.

She goes on to say:

I tried to live in the same way with my husband Joe and with Lori. I felt so blessed that I had her after all these years. My life was wrapped around the two of them, and I was the old-fashioned motherly type.

I had learned that from my mother, too.

I guess I would sum it up as there's nothing like family.

Agnes, it has been an absolute treasure to work with and learn from you. I am so honored to have been a part of this project and so thrilled that my father and our dear friend Ava are here with Dunreith and Aidan to join everyone here in wishing you a Happy 92nd Birthday, in congratulating you on your achievement, and in thanking you for your memory, your stories and your gift to all of us.

We thank you and we love you.

Please join me in raising our glasses to Agnes."

We toasted Agnes, we sang Happy Birthday to her and we drank the champagne Pinstripes had provided for us.

While we were doing so, we also drank in the special pleasure that comes from having worked hard on a major project of uncertain outcome, from not having given up and having emerged on the other side with a result in which we can all take pride.

Sitting there with my wife and father and son and dear friend, celebrating with friends and the family I had gotten to know, the six years all felt worthwhile.

For a moment, all felt right in my world.

ON MY TEACHER'S SHOULDERS LAUNCH EVENT

Nov. 18, 2012

Steve Doran (left) and me on the first day of school in 1974.
(Photo by Paul Tamburello)

We did it.

Close to 40 years after I watched him perform as Captain Hook and decided I wanted him as my teacher, more than a quarter century after I first worked in his classroom and nearly two decades after he learned that he had a degenerative neuromuscular condition, Paul Tamburello and I called together our communities to the school where we met and developed a lifelong friendship to celebrate the completion of our project, *On My Teacher's Shoulders.*

The book and website tell the story of my learning from Paul at three different stages in my life: as a fourth grade student; as an apprentice teacher; and as a young man seeking to emulate his example of resilience and service in the face of physical adversity.

During this time my relationship with him changed from student to apprentice to friend to fellow traveler on the road of life.

The names I have called him reflect that evolution.

With some difficulty, I learned to make the transition from "Mr. Tamburello" to "Paul," and then from "Paul" to "PT."

But one thing that our hundreds of conversations had taught me was that not only was Paul changed by receiving from me one of the largest possible pieces of evidence of teacherly impact possible. He also faced substantial questions at each of the junctures where he taught me.

Several years before he had me as a student in his classroom, Paul had been a first-year teacher struggling with the same insecurities he would guide me through nearly two decades later.

When I asked if I could teach in his classroom, he hesitated before agreeing. He was unsure whether my perception of him and the quality of his work would continue in the face of an extensive apprenticeship.

And when he was told that he did not have ALS, or Lou Gehrig's disease, he wrestled with how to manage an unknown encroaching physical limitation before resolving that the answer lay in helping to raise money and awareness about the disease he could have contracted.

Paul's reflections on each of these stages appear on the website.

Last night, in the auditorium where I went and performed as a student and worked as an adult, he read them.

The crowd was a gorgeous tapestry comprised of people from many different points in our lives. Time's passage and life's strains and stresses and habits of diet and sleep had etched their marks on all of us.

But we were there, gathering and hugging and nearly levitating the cafeteria before filing in and sitting on the lacquer-covered bleachers I had once sat on as a student and apprentice.

A tall, large screen stood in the middle of the room with a wooden podium with a microphone and silver metal plaque with the school's name.

Brandishing a silver tinfoil hook on the end of his left arm, Paul recreated the role of Captain Hook with gusto after I read the chapter's opening paragraphs.

We flowed back and forth as we took the audience through the journey.

Paul shared his hesitancy about my returning to his classroom before I read about parent-teacher conferences we conducted. After he detailed his response to learning he had Spinal Muscular Atrophy, I showed a local television clip from April 1999 about my running the Boston Marathon in Paul's honor.

I read from the book's final chapter before we turned to the audience:

After the ceremony was over, we all stood around, soaking in the evening's warmth. It was one of those moments where wine and food and company and good cheer and humor and history produced an enchanted air that descended from the ceiling and draped over all of us.

I didn't want it to end, but people started checking their watches and the round of goodbye hugs and promises to get together began.

Paul and I walked out together with Dunreith and Nona and Jon. The air was warm, the sky was clear and the stars glittered and shimmered above us.

We hugged each other one more time.

It was a hug that encapsulated fourth grade and the return visits and Mom and Dad's accident and working in his classroom and 10 Positive Spins and two marathons.

It was a hug that covered the 30 years since I had first seen him as Captain Hook to his rendition not an hour earlier.

It was a hug that covered the time from him being Mr. Tamburello to Paul to PT, from teacher to mentor to friend to fellow traveler on the road of life.

I looked at my wife and brother and gazed at the starry night and saw farther and wider than I ever had before.

We ended the presentation and reveled in the feeling of love that enveloped the room.

For me, the evening was the culmination of a project that I first began more than a dozen years ago to honor Paul Tamburello, a man who has been a vital force in my personal and professional growth and development.

It also was the manifestation of a vision of integrating a community and set of life experiences during the 47 years I have been privileged to live on this planet.

And, on the profoundest level, it was an affirmation of the possibility that there can be congruence between our deepest dream and values, our actions, the projects we undertake and complete, and our circle of loved ones.

We did it.

HARVARD PROGRAM IN REFUGEE TRAUMA POEM: HERE

Nov. 10, 2010

Here, in the long room,
With the green walls like curtains
And large mirrors ringed with gold,
With the three glass chandeliers
And the art on the pink cracked ceiling;
Here, in the lovely villa
With the gorgeous gardens and uneven ground
That provokes anxiety in some of us and
Is a reminder of history for all of us;
In our ideal city where we are the people
Where coffee is sacred
And lunch is holy;
Here, near the tombs of Lawrence's lovers of life,
Where women were citizens and queens,
We arrive on the bus
That winds through hilly green roads
Splashed with neat yellow rows of leaves
As the ancient walled city
With the cobble-stoned streets
And towering Duomo
Recedes, like a dream.
Here we gather,
Mostly women with a sprinkling of men,
From Kenya and South Africa and Uganda
and Egypt and the Sudan and Nigeria and Zimbabwe,

From Italy and England
From Chile and Argentina and Colombia and Brazil
From Canada and France
From Turkey and Switzerland and Greece
From India and the United States
And Cambodia and the Philippines and Lebanon
And Albania and Sweden and Haiti
And Iran and Afghanistan and Pakistan and Australia
And others I have not named or do not yet know.
Although we differ in age and race and
Disability and religion and paths behind us and journeys ahead of us,
We are united in our goals of seeking truth,
Of listening with an open heart so as to heal
And of caring for ourselves as we work.
Here we learn about the eight dimensions of the
Global Mental Health Action Plan
And add our own.
Here we do the hard and sometimes painful work of deep reflection,
Of seeking the inner way.
Here we speak with courage and listen with care.
We share where we are wounded but not broken.
Here
In the room
In the Villa
Near the tombs
We learn.
We hope.
We dream.
We plan.
We believe.
We can.
Here.

AN OPEN LETTER TO RED SOX FANS

Oct. 14, 2011

Dear fellow Red Sox fans,

Admit it.

Isn't this collapse just a little bit fun?

I mean, we've had an incredible run in the past decade with John, Larry, Theo and Terry.

Sure, it started with the agonizing Game 7 loss to the Yankees in 2003 when Grady Little left Pedro in too long and Aaron Boone, of all people, went yard in extra innings off of a valiant Tim Wakefield–a blow that led my brother Mike to call from California, and say, with absolutely no hint of irony or hyperbole, "The Holocaust. Rwanda. The Yankees over the Red Sox. Must evil always triumph over good?"

But the next year the self-described "bunch of idiots" did what no other club had ever done before in winning four straight from the same Yankees of A-Roid, Jeter and Matsui, then sweeping the Cardinals for the first championship in 86 years.

A retooled lineup got down 3-1 to the Cleveland Indians in 2007. Yet rather than believing the series was over, we felt we had the Indians right where we wanted them.

Seven games later, a second championship came.

Beyond the victories, the team moved over the years beyond the racist roots of the Red Sox, who were the last team to employ a black player and who were routinely listed as the least desirable club for black and Latino players.

To me, it all started coming a bit easy for us.

The bandwagon fans who joined the mythical "nation."

The endless spending that placed us in the very upper echelons of teams.

The arrogant expectation that we would simply win every year.

You see, I came up in the 70s and 80s. While there were a lot of adjectives you could use to describe Red Sox fans of our vintage, smug was not in the top 10.

I'd venture to say it wasn't in the top 100.

Insanely informed and knowledgeable? Yup.

Intensely passionate? Check.

Hoping against hope that things would work out, but somehow knowing that it would all come down in the end? You got it.

I grew up that way.

I turned 10 years old the night Carlton Fisk waved his Game 6 home run fair, then barged through the fans storming the field. It was a classic moment that lives on to this day, but the fact remains that Joe Morgan's Game 7 single won the series for the Reds, not us.

I was 12 going on 13 in the summer of '78.

I remember as if it was yesterday scoffing at my mother, a Brooklyn native, when she said in July the race was not over when the Sox were 13 games up on the Yankees.

I lived Bucky Dent and Yaz flying out to end the 5-4 playoff game with Rick "the Rooster" Burleson in scoring position.

I had just turned 21 the night that the hobbled Bill Buckner let Mookie Wilson's ground ball go through his legs. I knew then we didn't even need to watch Game 7, which, if you care to think about it, also saw the Red Sox take an early lead that we somehow knew would go away.

I remember the agony.

While it was tough, it was part of me.

It formed me, made me grittier, just that bit more skeptical toward the world.

This September has brought that back.

The Sox didn't just lose, they collapsed in unprecedented fashion, blowing a nine-game lead and playing .259 baseball the entire month.

The aftermath has been even uglier, as management has leaked unseemly details about Francona's life.

Former wunderkind Theo Epstein, another Brookline native, is apparently preparing to come here to Chicago to help another historic franchise break its curse.

And Big Papi, the ultimate Yankees slayer, is making approving comments about our enemies-a potential first step, some say, in what could be the ultimate betrayal.

It's been ugly.

It's been toxic.

Yet it's also gotten us back to our roots.

The epic failure revives some of the gut-level insecurity we carried with us for generations.

The ownership dysfunction brings back the worst of the Yawkeys and Haywood Sullivan era from the 30s to the 70s combined.

And, as always, the haunting specter of the Yankees looms.

Don't get me wrong.

I'm not happy we lost.

I think the way ownership treated Tito is reprehensible.

I'm definitely sorry to see Theo conclude he has to go.

But I am glad that the smugness is gone.

And, if we had to go down, I'm glad we did it in memorable and classic Red Sox fashion.

One of the questions Red Sox fans asked for generations was, "What will we do if we win?"

We've found out.

Now it's time for a different chapter.

I, for one, am excited.

I hope you are, too.

Jeff

THE MANY GIFTS OF AN ABUNDANT LIFE

July 28, 2012

Jeff and Dunreith Kelly Lowenstein
during a bike ride in early 2015.
(Photograph by
Jeff Kelly Lowenstein)

Being firmly (I think) in the middle of life, I find myself drawing far more than before on my own experience to understand life's events, time's passage and current moments.

It is and will always be true that all we have at any given moment is the present.

It is also true that, more and more, I understand the present in light of the past.

I have a different understanding and appreciation of how hard it is to conceive and carry out major life endeavors.

I'm talking about big stuff here.

Like raising a child or finishing a book or sharing a life.

Dunreith and I got married three times.

The first one on Labor Day 2000.

She, Aidan and I stood together in a park we all loved under a tree that he had chosen with three roots that came together at the base.

Before Justice of the Peace Bruce Zeitler declared us man and wife, the three of us, holding hands in a circle, moved through the ceremony we had designed.

We celebrated by going to Whole Foods and Interskate 91 to rollerblade.

The second ceremony, a public one, took place 11 years ago today.

We returned to Look Park, but this time invited about 165 friends and their 50 children.

The hors d'oeuvres were potluck.

Dunreith's friend Janet brought the flowers.

Our friend Carole, whose daughter had died of cancer the month before just shy of 30 years old and left three young girls behind, baked the cakes.

Dad and Diane brought a case of white wine.

And Helen, my beautiful, beloved mother-in-law, after deliberately hanging back for months of planning, crammed more activity into the last three days than I ever could have imagined.

Dunreith, her father Marty, Helen and I were at our apartment in Easthampton before driving to the ceremony in the same park.

Tired from all the preparations, I laid back on the couch on the first floor for just a minute.

"Enjoy it, Jeff, because tomorrow it'll all be over," Marty said.

He was right.

Helen prepared her only daughter for her walk down the aisle, and the three of them drove to Look Park in Cracker Curran's vintage Ford convertible. Sitting in the front seat caused Marty's balky knees to go halfway down his throat, but not so far down that you couldn't hear his particularly hearty "Jesus Christ" in the next state.

But he kept driving.

Nothing would stop him from giving his daughter the day she wanted to have.

The two of them walked Dunreith down the aisle, too.

Helen started an impromptu acapella version of "Here Comes the Bride" as they took the final steps before handing her symbolically and physically to me.

Bruce Zeitler opened the ceremony by saying, "It is a pleasure to be here once again in Look Park to marry Dunreith and Jeff."

Mom read a poem she had written about us that concluded "The future looks good" before Bruce once more pronounced us man and wife.

Spencer Schock, a friend from freshman year at Stanford, married his lovely bride Heather on the same day.

This morning, 11 years later, we spoke.

He and Heather have made a life in Spencer's hometown of Bend, Oregon and are raising their four children together.

Spencer and I mixed catching up on parenting, work and finances with references to humorous moments during our freshman year misadventures.

Today, while Dunreith took a walk with our dear friend Cheryl, I drove downtown to pick up my computer and do some analysis on a new dataset I received on Thursday.

Mom and I spoke on the way down, and she filled me in on the Olympics' opening ceremony.

After I returned, Dunreith and I went on a long, rambling bike ride, heading farther north than we had ever gone before. The sky was clear blue with streaks of white clouds, the air was pure and we felt that we could do the 100-mile ride we have planned for two months from now today.

We stopped at the post office to mail the photos, video and audio commentaries to Russ Weller, the web designer who will help me move my book about former fourth grade teacher, mentor and friend Paul Tamburello to completion.

A few miles later, at the Starbucks in Glencoe, we bought a coffee and mocha frappuccino with whipped cream, savoring every last extravagant morsel of sugar and caffeine.

Then we biked north in earnest, ending up in Highwood, one of the state's few majority-Latino populations. I walked into Nueva Imagen, a beauty salon, and chatted with Isidro, the owner and a Colombian who opened the place two-and-a-half years ago after working for someone else for a decade and a half.

When Dunreith and I were dating, she lived in Easthampton and I was in Boston. We talked every night. Among other things, it was the easy, intimate flow of conversation we shared that, for the first time in my life, made me feel that a romantic relationship I was involved in would never end.

The ride home was filled with that same kind of conversation I have always treasured. I shot hoops outside in our backyard for a little while, hearing the soothing sound of the ball passing through the net's metal chains as my body once again answered the call of repeating the motion I have done hundreds of thousands of times during the past 40 years.

We ate some dinner and watched the latest series we are enjoying together. As I do nearly every night these days, I made popcorn, letting the canola oil roll around the bottom of the pan to make sure it was covered before filling the bottom and then some with the hard orange kernels.

Then I sat down to write this.

Much has changed in the past 11 years.

Marty and Diane left us in 2010.

Helen passed away last September.

Aidan is no longer a boy, but a young man with a full beard, deep voice, broad shoulders and his own decisions.

But what has not changed is the accuracy of what Marty said to me on our wedding day.

That truth can be extended to our life as a whole: At one point, it will be over.

But what is also true is that, if you allow yourself to do so, you can soak in almost unimaginable joy and gratitude from the memory of a public commitment based on present and betting on future love, from the pleasure of riding 25 miles with that same woman, from laying the latest layer of a lifetime connection with family and friends, from the great gift of knowing what I love to do and giving myself the space to do so, and from the knowledge that we are working together to define and shape the life we want to live and to have lived.

Love.

Section II

LOSS

TRIBUTE TO BEAUTY TURNER

Dec. 24, 2008

Beauty Turner called herself a "writer and a fighter" for years.
(Photo by Jon Lowenstein/NOOR)

A lot of people talk about giving voice to the voiceless; Beauty Turner lived it everyday.

She did it in many ways, and did it with class and grace and heaping amounts of generosity.

She radiated inner and outer beauty, dressing elegantly and always treating people with dignity and respect. Her style showed how you could start with so little and end up carrying yourself like a queen without losing a common touch.

The youngest of 16 siblings, Beauty came up hard, survived and ended an abusive marriage, and eventually discovered a mission she embraced with gusto.

"I'm a writer and a fighter," she declared on the front page of *The Wall Street Journal* and to anyone she met.

The two were related, and she gave herself completely to both.

For years her writing was published in *Residents' Journal*, a publication by, for and about residents of public housing. It was the premier source of stories about the community.

In its pages Beauty wrote stories that garnered national awards and showed that the Chicago Housing Authority's claims of a smooth "Plan for Transformation" were anything but that and that the pronouncements of politicians like Mayor Richard M. Daley were often a bunch of self-serving hype and lies.

"Deadly Moves," a collaboration with *The Chicago Reporter*, revealed that the drop in the city's murder rate was not caused by effective community policing, as Daley maintained. Rather it came from the moving of the people from public housing to suburban communities, where the number of killings rose.

Beauty also wrote for *South Street Journal* for years; and, after her departure from *Residents' Journal*, on her blog.

Writing was just one part of Beauty's repertoire.

She was the driving force in a video Sudhir Venkatesh made about some of the last people to live in the Robert Taylor Homes.

She hosted a cable television show earlier this year.

She created the highly successful *Ghetto Bus Tours* in which visitors of all ages and backgrounds from the city, from the suburbs, from across the country and even around the world learned about and listened to residents of public housing telling their stories.

Her fighting also took many forms.

There was the public work she did, like attending community meetings, speaking up at public events and participating in marches.

But she also constantly did unheralded work that was no less central to her mission.

I saw this in the summer of 2007, when I was getting started on an investigation of fatal police shootings in Chicago.

My brother Jon, Beauty and I were planning to go to a press conference on the West Side, but had to make a stop at the federal building first. Distraught about a legal difficulty, a woman had locked herself in the bathroom and refused to leave.

In her loving manner, Beauty spoke to the younger woman, advised her and coaxed her out of the room.

"You are the only one who came," the woman said, tears streaming down her face when she finally emerged.

Beauty hugged the woman, connected her to a lawyer and let her know it would be all right. Other community organizations had said they would be there, but Beauty was the one who showed the woman she was on her side.

We missed the meeting, but the action had moved to the police station. On a "work schedule," I headed back to the office, but Beauty kept right on going. She didn't stop until the early morning, when she rested for a few hours and then started the same cycle all over again.

Her actions inspired a song by young men and made her the subject of magazine cover stories and a key figure in multiple documentary films. Beauty soaked in all the affirmation like a warm bath but never forgot who she was or what she was about.

Where most of the outside world looked at the Robert Taylor Homes and saw crime and violence and poverty and a symbol for all that could and had gone wrong in public housing, Beauty saw family and community and people she would do anything for.

No one was better connected to people in the city's public housing.

No one had a purer relationship with the people on whose behalf she worked.

No one worked harder and listened better.

In short, she loved what she did and the people with whom she worked.

Love is critical to include when reflecting on Beauty because talking only about her actions and accomplishments misses a central part of her essence. Coupled with a hunger for justice, love was her life's driving force as well as her most common greeting.

I never saw her call anyone anything but "love." (I didn't take her up on her offer one day to meet Mayor Daley, so I don't know how that would have turned out.)

In many ways, Beauty was getting launched on her own.

A split with *Residents' Journal* after many years had been painful, but she had emerged speaking well of her former colleagues. The ghetto and gallery tours had been rousing successes. Her children were doing well and she was working on a book about her life.

She was seemingly midway through her life's journey and flourishing.

Which is why her death hurts so much.

In the week before she died, Beauty wrote a piece for our publication's blog about Barack Obama's election.

In the piece, she recounted dreaming about being back in slavery with prominent black leaders like Frederick Douglass, Sojourner Truth and others.

"They told me it was time," she wrote. "The red blood of our ancestors was crying out from the ground for justice. We danced around flickering candles to the beat of a drum-a Ngoma with the ancestors."

In Beauty's vision, Obama emerged in the 21st century, eliciting a loud cheer from the people. The three days of rain that followed represented the tears of the people who had been enslaved.

She concluded:

"The ancestors told me to keep him focused concerning the plight of the poor and to tell him, 'Forget not from which you came!'

Mr. Obama, all eyes of the nations are focused on you; so stay focused on the mission that was ordained by God, which he has laid upon you to do!

Be a president not just for some of the people but for all."

This was vintage Beauty: the dream, the connection with the ancestors, the joy of the victory, and her mission of urging those in power to remember the powerless.

Now she is gone, and we are much the poorer for it.

Chicago and the world became a little less brave and a lot less fun on Thursday. Beauty's death leaves a gaping hole in the city and among the community of people who strive to leave the world better than we found it.

Of course the love she spread and the message of her life will be remembered and honored and heeded by those of us who knew and loved her. Of course her writing and actions and advocacy will endure in all of us.

Still, the loss is undeniable and heartbreaking.

Thank you, Beauty, for your life.

Thank you for your gifts.

Thank you for your example.
Thank you for your love.
We will miss you. We respect you. And we love you.

RIP, MARTY KELLY

March 27, 2010

My father-in-law Martin Kelly in his favorite chair at his home in Wilbraham, Massachusetts.
(Photograph by Jeff Kelly Lowenstein)

We all knew this day was coming, but somehow you're never quite prepared for the loss of someone as vital and memorable as Marty.

He was born in Pittsfield, but was a Springfield man through and through. Reared in Hungry Hill, he graduated from Classical High School in 1950 and was AIC Class of 1954. Had my mother-in-law Helen not insisted, Marty might well have happily spent the rest of his life at 2197 Wilbraham Road in the city of his childhood.

He loved hotdogs and beans and was a steak and potatoes man who went heavy on the salt even after his septuple bypass in 1998. He treasured his afternoon Dewar's and Russell Stover jellybeans, even when they stuck to his teeth. He dressed nattily and wore his hats and ties well.

Politically, he was pure red in one of the country's bluest states. We eventually surfaced, if not vigorously discussed, our differences in that area. Marty was very tolerant. I believe his understanding came in part because he expected little different from his daughter's husband, in part because he met some of my friends and may have found me reasonable by comparison, and in part because he had the ability to, in the words of Atticus Finch, walk around in another man's shoes.

He worked at different jobs over the years, and, for Marty, life was never about work.

For him, life came down to three central, deep-rooted and related passions: family, friends and golf, though not always, it might seem, in that order.

Golf got a hold of him as a teenager and never left go.

It was no accident that all of Marty's grandchildren called him Par. Golf took Marty across the country and led to thousands of hours of pleasure and hearty doses of frustration, years as a Massachusetts Golf Association official, and, for me as a son-in-law, a perpetual question whenever the conversation seemed to be flagging or heading in a contentious direction: "What do you think of Tiger Woods?"

But Marty's endless desire to improve, his quest for the perfect swing, the flawless hole–he could recite by memory what Garry Brown wrote about a hole in one he shot–and the unblemished round, were just a part of his love for the game.

His was a shared passion.

The Friday games he orchestrated by tinkering constantly with the foursomes gave him weekly pleasure. As the round's architect, he often invoked his design privileges to make sure that he ended up with Tommy Henshon. Although he was not always enamored of Tommy's methods of coaching and encouragement, he invariably spoke about him and his game with admiration.

"He knows how to make the putts when it matters," Marty told me.

Regardless of the result, Marty and the other players would go out for a meal and drinks to mark the occasion, begin the weekend and start to prepare for the next week's game.

Golf and friendship also intersected with one of Marty's longest-standing friends, Eugene Mulcahy.

Gene, Marty and Helen spent several winters together chasing the white ball in the Carolinas together. While the relationship did have occasional moments of tension, Marty would end each description of Gene's alleged wrongdoings with the statement, "Of course, he may not find me the easiest person to get along with, either."

He did get along with his family, though.

For Marty, family first meant his parents, Grammy and Poppy, and his siblings Bill, Dave, Dick and Ginna. They dipped and coated him in the Kelly brand of love that breeds strong and self-respecting personalities, the kind that let you know that you are claimed and accepted and loved for who you are.

Later, family meant Helen, the bright and beautiful cheerleading daughter of Polish immigrants who hailed from Enfield, Connecticut. They made a striking couple. He was lean and lanky and broad-shouldered, with an athletic gait, genial smile and affable wit. She was elegant, composed and always well put together. They fit well on each other's arm.

They didn't just look good, but together they shared a lifetime of children, caring for and burying their parents, working and retiring, the birth and growth of grandchildren, family vacations, travel, and then the twilight years.

Family also meant his three children, all of whom he accepted completely and loved fiercely. His kids were a constant source of delight. He spoke about them with a combination of pride and wonder that he had had something to do with the full-fledged people he had helped create.

Like the time at my bachelor party, when, after driving us in from Western Mass. and happily settling into a beer, he turned to me and declared, "Dunreith's a tiger, Jeff, and if you don't know it by now, it's too late for you."

I assured him I was familiar with his only daughter's fiery nature and we laughed before finishing our drinks.

He'd do anything for Dunreith.

When we got married for the second time at Look Park in July 2001, Dunreith wanted to arrive in Cracker Curran's vintage Ford convertible. Sitting in the front seat caused Marty's balky knees to go halfway down his throat, but not so far down that you couldn't hear his particularly hearty "Jesus Christ" in the next state.

But he kept driving.

Nothing would stop him from giving his daughter the day she wanted to have.

I will say that he started to draw the line later that year when we got married for a third time in a Jewish ceremony the day before our first anniversary–an event that made Marty miss his beloved Labor Day golf tournament.

After the ceremony ended, he said, without a hint of humor, "That's enough. You can do this again. But if it's on Labor Day, count me out."

We never tested him on that one.

He and Helen flew out to Chicago for Dunreith's surprise 45th birthday party and, even though he was failing, again for her 50th.

Family meant Aidan, Dylan, Colin, Jacob, Sarah and Regan, his six grandchildren. He adored all of them, and would finish every conversation about them by saying, "They're good kids."

Family meant in-laws and nieces and nephews and cousins.

Fortunately, family meant me, too.

Marty took a little while to get that my last name then was Lowenstein, not Weinstein. But he got there and stayed there. He welcomed me into the family from the moment we got engaged. Dunreith and I went over to 11 Ridgewood, where she showed her new ring to her mother. We looked at old family pictures and some childhood report cards.

"You're two people with an idea and you're doing something about it," Marty said.

He was right, and we did.

In addition to giving me a major gift by introducing me to speed reading, Marty gave me the gift of perspective. When we were at our apartment in Easthampton preparing to go over to Look Park for the wedding, he told me, in essence, "Enjoy it, Jeff, because tomorrow it'll all be over."

Marty encouraged me as a husband and father by including me in family events, by asking me about the roles I was beginning to inhabit and by leaving the three of us alone to forge our lives together.

The end was hard.

Marty knew until recently what he was losing and it frustrated him a lot. Still, we had moments of clarity and connection on the phone.

I'm proud to be part of a family where the woman he spent his life with and the children he helped raise showed him the same kind of love he had given to them.

Helen never flinched or complained as the dementia advanced. Shaun always answered the calls his parents placed. Josh spent hours and hours working to get the best legal, medical and financial support for his father as Rebecca's pregnancy advanced to its final weeks. And Dunreith came back from Chicago again and again and again. Along with the support of Cathy, Rebecca and the community Helen and Marty had created throughout their lives, they shared the load and worked to make the end of his life as peaceful as possible.

Now it has come.

We are sad that Marty is gone.

I cried several times in the hours before his passing on Friday, knowing what was coming, but not when. Yet, in our sadness, I hope we can take consolation in knowing he is still with us, and always will be.

I'll think of him when I'm writing this blog, which is predicated on reading, when I'm telling people about speed reading, or when I'm watching Tiger Woods re-emerge from his self-imposed exile and try to win the Masters again.

I'll think of him when I'm sitting next to his chair in front of the grandfather clock at the head of the table where we had so many meals together.

I'll think about the conversations we had and the memories we shared.

I'll be grateful.

And I'll smile.

Marty, I thank you. I'll miss you. And I love you.

EULOGY FOR DIANE LOWENSTEIN

July 5, 2010

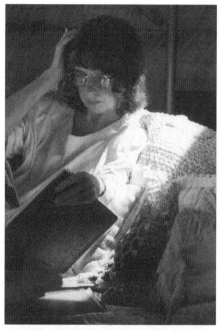

My late stepmother, Diane Lowenstein,
writing poetry in Rockport.
(Photo courtesy of Ed Lowenstein)

Good morning.

I am Jeff Kelly Lowenstein, one of Diane's stepsons. I knew her for more than 35 years, starting when her oldest son Alex and I were in a joint second/third grade classroom. It's nearly impossible to encapsulate such a vital and dynamic person as Diane. But when talking and thinking about her with Dunreith and Aidan in preparation for talking today, several major traits stood out to us.

Diane was a marvelous listener.

Beyond the training she had as a counselor, she had a deep empathic sense forged during her years in Luxembourg after World War II. It let her make the person she was speaking with feel safe and allowed her to listen to what a person was saying, what they meant, what they felt. She also could connect how whatever they were discussing related to the person's life as a whole. Dad has talked to me often about how he had lived 52 years before feeling completely understood by another person.

Diane gave that to him.

Her listening was a central part of why he felt that way. Dunreith treasured the walks and excursions she and Diane took in Evanston, in Cambridge and in Rockport for that same quality. Running the gamut from children to George Eliot, their conversations were often punctuated by hearty chuckles on both sides.

Diane was enormously generous.

I am confident that all of us experienced and benefited from the example of Diane's unstinting generosity toward those she knew and loved–her family, friends and circle of intimates–and those she was just meeting for the first time. Dunreith talked about asking Diane why she had so much loose change in the Cambridge house: her response was so that she could share what she had with people who needed it. Beyond her material sharing, Diane could not have been more welcoming and inclusive toward the three of us as a family from the moment she met Dunreith and Aidan.

She had a wonderful sense of occasion.

I used to live at a community service center in rural Kentucky, where the father of the family once told me, "I don't have much, Jeff, but I live rich."

Diane definitely lived rich, making sure that her children had enough money for popcorn at the movies during lean financial times and telling Aidan that he could get one of every kind of candy in Tuck's. (Years later he described the experience as one of his life's greatest moments.) From calling Dunreith mid-day at Facing History and saying, "Ha, ha, you're at work and I'm not," to sipping white wine while watching a sunset at the Headlands in Rockport, Diane treated every day as cause for celebration.

She showed this sensibility on a rainy weekday night in July 1990.

Dad and Diane cooked an 18-pound turkey that they packed up with some Brie cheese, potato chips and matzah to deliver to Fenway Park, where my partner and I were selling Green Monster t-shirts. Having tried with very little success during the previous month to establish my street cred on Lansdowne Street, I have to admit that the sight of my slightly giddy father and stepmother lugging a basket filled with these goodies did not initially fill me with either joy or excitement.

But then the street's vendors and passersby swarmed our stand and devoured the food with grateful ferocity. Sal, a homeless gentleman who informed me the chips were stale, was the only exception.

On the other hand, the members of a nearby sausage stand instantly proclaimed it the best meal they had ever eaten. Three years later, when my brother Jon worked the same job, he would field occasional hopeful queries from the other vendors about the arrival of another turkey.

Diane just laughed the whole time.

Diane's laughter encompassed many of the qualities I have just described. She had a robust laugh that erupted from within, subsumed her entire person and lasted for minutes on end.

Diane laughed at the silliness of situations, like when I got a $275 ticket and my car towed at O'Hare Airport after running in to pick her and Dad up at the baggage claim. Now, honesty does compel me to say that Dad found the moment a tad less humorous as he followed Diane's instructions and pulled out his credit card to pay the man in the towing lot. Diane acted like this was the funniest thing she had ever seen.

She laughed with and about her family, which was her biggest source of joy. In addition to spending time with family members, she loved to tell stories about us.

Like about the time her grandson Max, after observing his father, kept hitting his hands on a desk and repeating, "Damnit, damnit, damnit."

When asked what he was doing, Max replied, "I'm working."

But she also laughed as a statement of defiance during all her years of medical difficulty.

Diane was remarkably courageous and unfailingly positive during her lengthy and increasingly challenging ordeal. Drawing strength from the tradition of strong women in her family that included her mother and her Aunt Clara, both of whom she revered, she would chuckle when you would inquire about her health and then turn the conversation to how you were doing.

Deeply held values about what and who mattered in life underpinned Diane's actions–beliefs about the centrality of family, friends and faith; about recognizing and embracing life's occasionally absurd nature; and, even when times are really hard, maintaining an upbeat and giving attitude.

Diane had wisdom and strength and courage and perspective, and we are better and richer for the qualities and the gift of her presence. Dad was like a flower who bloomed during the nearly quarter century that he spent with his Honeybunch, becoming a better husband, father, friend and man. And I would suggest that Diane enriched all of our lives. That is why we are all here to honor her, and why, even though we mourn her physical passing, we draw comfort in knowing that her laughter, generosity, and spirit are with us now and forever.

Diane, we thank you.

We miss you.

And we love you.

RIP, HELEN KELLY

Sept. 27, 2011

Helen C. Kelly spread love throughout her 79 years of life.
(Photograph courtesy of the Kelly family)

We all knew this moment was coming, and somehow it still is hard to fully accept that it's here.

helen C. Kelly, born Helena Chmielewski, my elegant, intelligent, strong, endlessly giving mother-in-law, died at home and surrounded by family as she wished. She was 79 years old, or, as she liked to say, in her eightieth year.

During her childhood in a cold-water flat in Enfield, Connecticut, this daughter of Polish immigrants absorbed lessons of hard work, the centrality of family and the importance of savoring all of life's experiences. From her family she also learned about honesty, integrity, self-reliance and the tenacity to not give up on what she wanted.

Helen always remembered what it was like to grow up not having much, and she carried an unwavering generosity with her throughout her life.

She was one of the most giving people I ever met.

She gave in so many different ways.

To the world she gave the beauty that saw her named head cheerleader and Tobacco Valley Queen, that led the quarterback of the football team to ask permission to date her and that, in the early 50s, caught the eye of a lean, lanky and gallant young man from Hungry Hill via Pittsfield named Marty Kelly.

We know where that went.

Helen retained her beauty throughout her life, her figure slender, her hair perfectly coiffed after her weekly trip to Angel's shop, her nails and jewelry just so. Even at Marty's funeral last year, two classmates from the Enfield years came and you could tell they still saw the younger woman in the setting sun they saw before them, and liked both equally. Helen's beauty was not just physical, of course, but in how she carried herself with such a dignified grace.

Helen gave to the children of Springfield with whom she worked tirelessly for 30 years in many of the city's poorest neighborhoods. She started as a teacher and made her way up the ranks, working the last decade of her career as a principal.

Helen gave to her lady friends, with whom she lunched and golfed and laughed and discussed books and went to Florida and to whom she listened with compassion and without judgment to their stories of children and husbands and grandchildren, of ailments, defeats and triumphs.

Above all, though, she gave to family.

Helen treasured each one of her family members, from her parents Gladys and Anthony to her sister Binkie, her niece Pam and her family, to Marty and the three kids, her in-laws and her seven grandchildren.

Our son Aidan once called her the perfect grandmother, and he was right. Helen was everything a Babci should be–kind, ceaselessly generous, never ruffled, willing to dispense advice when necessary, always claiming and loving Aidan, Dylan, Colin, Jacob, Regan, Sarah and Lucy with a gentle fierceness.

When she received her diagnosis in late May, Helen did not sit around Western Massachusetts and start treatment. Instead she boarded a plane with Dunreith and flew out to Chicago, where she watched Aidan get ready for his prom and graduate from high school. She needed a little help walking around and sitting in the stands for hours during the ceremony wasn't easy, but Helen neither complained nor missed a second.

Nothing was going to keep her from seeing her oldest grandson dressed up in a tux and receiving the diploma that marked the end of his childhood and his readiness to go out into the world.

She not only gave life to Shaun, Dunreith and Josh, she also gave them the gift of permission to truly be themselves. Those of you who have met any of them for even a short period know that she succeeded in that. Their individuality can make for lively discussion and an assertive decision-making process, and Helen wouldn't have it any other way.

Helen transmitted a basic level of confidence, of unconditional acceptance that let you know you were seen and cherished and one of hers. She'd also let you know gently but firmly if you were stepping over the line, always conveying an unshakeable love that emanated from within her core.

Fortunately, to Helen, family meant me, too.

We had a mutual admiration society in which we would slowly chant the words "Num-ber One" to each other three times on the phone, punctuated by a whoop.

Helen encouraged me throughout our courtship and marriage, during our morning chats to start the day, in the supportive cards she wrote and sent on expected and unexpected occasions, in the blue sweater she sent when I got my first job as a reporter with benefits, and in how she gave Dunreith, Aidan and me the space we needed to build our lives together. All of our interactions were encased in her base level confidence that I could face and meet the challenges in front of me.

Helen told me she believed in me, and I am a better husband, father and man because of her many gifts.

Yet as much as she gave to others, she also gave to herself.

Helen had a tremendous ability to experience pleasure in the moment, whether drinking a late afternoon Scotch with Marty, looking at a bird that had flown near her window at 11 Ridgewood, using her sturdy fingers and strong wrist to extract every last morsel of lobster from a claw and leg while we were in Maine, listening to a Tom Waits song, sharing a bag of chips with Dunreith, holding Lucy while visiting with Josh and Rebecca, shopping at Brimfield with Shaun and caring for his three children, and so many more.

Like the time at a family wedding, when, after a couple of drinks, she danced and walked around with a flower clenched between her teeth-a combination that prompted Marty to say, "Oh, boy."

Or, just a few a weeks ago, when she came to after her appendix surgery, looked at Josh and Shaun, her two grown sons, and said, repeatedly, "What a party."

That was Helen.

She gave herself the gift of travel, to Chicago many times with Marty to visit us, and, with Dunreith, to Israel, Germany and Poland, her family's homeland that she had never seen.

She also gave herself and us the example of a life in which she did not give up on her heartfelt desires.

Some people advised her not to get a driver's license. But she did it.

She not only went back to school while a mother of two to earn her undergraduate degree, she later went on to earn a Master's besides.

She could have stayed in the classroom, but she served the last 10 years of her career as a principal.

Helen continued giving until the very end.

In the week before she died, Dunreith put me on speaker phone. I did our little chant, but not too loudly, then told her I loved her.

"Love you, too," her voice came back, a little scratchy but unmistakably clear.

Finally, Helen gave us the gift of how she died.

She chose to go home and be with her family, ready for, and unafraid of, what would come afterward.

"When the carriage shuts down, the ride is over," she said at one point in the hospital. "It's time to stop."

And she did, with Dunreith and Shaun and Josh all working together to honor her wish to spend her final days at home.

Helen's death was in total keeping with how she lived and made me again appreciate in a different way the wonder and privilege of having known her.

Helen gave and gave and gave.

Because she gave and how she lived, thousands of children who might not otherwise have done so can read and have sought adventure in the world.

Because she gave, family and friends alike can walk around knowing they are loved and can realize their deepest dreams.

Because she gave, we are all here and know that we will carry her with us.

The love Helen gave and how she lived came back to her over and over, through Dunreith spending months in Western Massachusetts the last summer of her mother's life, through Shaun and Josh doing whatever they could to be there for Helen, and through the whole family getting together at Larry and Ginna's on July 4th weekend and one last time in Rockport, where everyone ate lobster, went to the beach, bowled and drank in each other's company.

Thank you, Helen.

Thank you, #1.

I thank you.

I will miss you.

I love you.

RIP, GAIL D'ANGELO AKA ANNIABBI

October 31, 2015

Gail D'Angelo with her son Vinnie,
my best friend in high school.
(Photo courtesy of the D'Angelo family)

If you're lucky, and I mean very lucky, you have a second mother like Gail D'Angelo.

Pete, the third of her four boys, and I were in the same homeroom. He wore an "I'm a Pepper" t-shirt to soccer tryouts and instantly impressed everyone with his skill. (I didn't make the team.)

Pete became my closest friend in high school and I spent a lot of time at the D'Angelo's home on Tappan Street.

What a home it was.

The family had already lived in Denver, Atlanta, Memphis and Houghton by the time they arrived in Brookline in 1979. These transitions and times in remote areas like Michigan's Upper Peninsula had helped form vicelike bonds between family members, but the truth is they would have been tight wherever they lived.

"We were always embraced and told we were loved," Pete once told me. I grew up not always having that feeling, so was drawn like so many others to their house.

Six o'clock meal times were sacred.

Pete talked about how he and James, in the midst of tightly contested basketball games at Dean Park, upon finding out that it was 5 minutes shy of dinner, would leave without compunction and sprint as fast as they could to make it home on time to consume the latest batch of Mrs. D's legendary red sauce.

The D'Angelos watched television together in the living room, and the heart of the home was the long wooden dining room table, site of many epic conversations.

You better have an opinion and come ready to defend it.

Any topic was fair game.

Had there ever been even a 12-year period in American history in which the nation had been true to its lofty creed? Did gay and lesbian people make things better or more difficult for themselves by protesting? Was it legitimate to miss the wedding of the daughters of one of Dr. D'Angelo's closest friends for very good seats at a Patriots exhibition game with and courtesy of Sam Matz?

In issues of art, the ultimate question was whether you would hang the artist's work on your wall.

All were debated in passionate and vigorous fashion in conversations that lasted hours. While there was plenty of posturing, yelling and more than a few insults thrown into the mix, there was at base a core commitment to seeking a higher level of understanding through dialogue, a quest for truth.

A series of guests sat at the table. One night could bring Neil Lempert, one of Dr. D's oldest and closest childhood friends from Astoria. Another could bring Boston University colleagues like Tony Mavretic. And a third could bring All-American Venezuelan soccer player Che Che Vidal.

All were welcomed into the fabric of D'Angelo family life.

The result was easily the most creative incubator I have ever had the privilege to experience. Cartoons, painting, sculpture, pottery, rap music delivered by The Goats, tampon cases, t-shirt businesses, books and movies—all emerged from conversations at 338 Tappan Street and the home of Henry and Gail D'Angelo.

Her gentle face framed by round glasses, Mrs. D. was at the core of it. Her kindness radiated out from her center and suffused her being with tenderness. Her greeting on the phone, "Hi, dear," always conveyed a love that enveloped you and made you feel cared about, seen and safe. She and Dr. D'Angelo taught their four boys to be fully themselves, to know that family meant most, and to cultivate their unique gifts and talents. All three parts stuck, and the boys have grown into husbands and fathers who have loved their children and wives in the same fierce way Dr. and Mrs. D. did during their quarter century of marriage.

She tended to Dr. D faithfully and without complaint during the four years after he was diagnosed with chronic leukemia. Along with Gioia, the boys' Sicilian grandmother, she was right next to him as he took his final breath in the home and with the family the two of them had made.

I offered to leave so they could all be alone.

She refused.

"You are one of us," she said.

I ran the Boston Marathon in Dr. D's honor just over two weeks later.

I had spoken with Mrs. D. before the race and said I might pass by their home around 3:00 p.m.

She was there just at the time, standing atop the wall near Star Market at the intersection of Beacon and Tappan Street.

She waved wordlessly to me.

I was cramping and had been doing a combination of walking and running for the previous 4 miles, but I kept going. Her silent reminder of why I was running helped me finish.

Dr. D's death marked the beginning for me of Mrs. D's next phase, one in which she moved out in the world, returning to and developing her artistic pursuits. A Batik artist when she was younger, she very well may have gotten there anyway, but I always felt that losing the only man she had loved that way at a comparatively young age made her bolder and braver.

This new period led to some seriously zany moments.

Like the time she announced years before any of the boys had wives or children that she wanted her grandmother name to be "Scissors" and proceeded to elaborate on her decision-making process and the benefits of what she had chosen.

Or when she came downstairs to do a line-by-line reading of a song she had written in neat cursive letters on white lineless paper called, "I'm an over-50 white mother rapper."

Or when she heard Vinnie's friend Randy Kolovsky bang away on the guitar at the basement, turned to the rest of us at the dinner table and declared, "He's really fighting it down there."

In her art, Mrs. D. took on the theme of the housedress. She subverted the era in which she had been raised and represented the dress in a less constraining and confining way.

Her work gained her mention in *The New York Times*, where a reviewer described her "The 1st to Last Homemade Housedress" as "a tissue-paper sewing pattern with elaborate instructions for embroidering sexist vulgarities in strategic locations."

She won recognition from national women's art organizations and earned fellowships at prestigious art colonies like MacDowell in North Carolina and Ragdale in Lake Forest.

In an article for a MacDowell newsletter Mrs. D. described herself as an inveterate piler, concluding that "If MacDowell is about anything, it's about the primacy of the artist's work space. I have, for my own mental health and enrichment, kept that lesson going in my own home. Give or take a pizza box."

She wrote these words and did her work under the name Anni Abbi.

In this regard she was only following her children. For the additional hook vocal we shared for the song "TV Cops" on Goats' debut album, *Tricks of the Shade*, Paul William D'Angelo became Paul Diesel. After a trip to South Africa in which he danced on the streets of Soweto, Gus morphed into Gazzi. Pete turned into Vinnie Angel and then Vinnie the Tamponcase Salesman. James had so many different names stretching back to high school that you couldn't come close to remembering them all, and I have a pretty good memory. (Think Oatie of the Goaties, Tommy Rome and Jaimito Situchi for starters.)

Mrs. D. came to Lake Forest shortly after Dunreith, Aidan and I had moved to Evanston.

I saw her work and we drove in to watch the July 4 fireworks that cascaded over Lake Michigan with my family.

Then, as always, she gave me the same affirmation, this time as a husband and father.

She had done that for years.

Before Dunreith, Aidan and I had ventured west from Massachusetts, we spent parts of three summers at the D'Angelo's small, rustic red cabin that abutted Cushman Pond in Center Lovell, Maine. We'd canoe around the pond, play Lego soccer, bury Aidan in the sand at the nearby beach and eat freshly cooked lobster every night. We've gone to a lot of places as a family since then, and Center Lovell still remains near the very top of treasured, peaceful memories.

I'd call every so often after we moved to Chicago.

Even though we didn't see each other as much, the connection was the same.

Mrs. D. was always encouraging, her voice carrying the same love and care.

We last saw each other at a book launch event in the auditorium of Pierce School in 2012. The Alzheimer's had already started its relentless, inexorable advance, but she knew who and where she was, and was happy and grateful to be there with James, his lovely wife Ronah and their son, Enrico, named for her late husband.

Gail.

Anniabbi.

Mrs. D., my beautiful, gentle, feisty, endlessly-loving second mother.

Thank you for giving my childhood best friend and his brothers life.

Thank you for helping me become a husband, father and man.

Although your passing brings us great grief, we are deeply grateful for the nearly 50 years and countless moments we shared with you and for all that you gave us by how you lived.

Love,

Jeff

RIP, GARY ADELMAN

Jan. 2, 2012

In news that brought me sadness and relief, I learned today that Gary Adelman, Mom's oldest cousin, died yesterday at age 76.

The source of my sadness is obvious.

Gary was one of the most courageous and vital people I ever met, and I loved him deeply.

Blinded after a case of childhood diabetes, he was a voracious, passionate and insightful consumer of literature who taught English at the University of Illinois, Urbana-Champaign for more than 40 years and who kept writing until the very end of his life.

His final book, this one about Beckett's heirs, will be published later this year. Gary wanted desperately to see it in print, but his body didn't make it.

He never complained about the impositions the disease caused him, instead seeking constantly to emphasize the positive parts of his life.

It lasted close to 30 years more than many had predicted.

After receiving his mother's kidney at age 44–he called it a gift of life twice given–he was expected to survive five years at the most.

Aunt Estelle's kidney functioned for 22 years.

Then, in a remarkable coincidence, Gary's wife Phyllis was also a kidney match. She gave him one of hers, and it helped him make it through nearly another decade.

These medical developments aside, and despite living the vast majority of his adult life in the Midwest, Gary never lost touch with his Brooklyn Jewish roots.

He was an Adelman through and through: bawdy, eager to engage in verbal combat with the goal of higher levels of understanding, and often equating volume with quality of argument.

In short, he was a vivid and unforgettable presence.

Mom always talked about how Gary got lit by literature while at Columbia University.

The fire never went out.

Gary came of age intellectually during an era before post-modernism had fully gotten its hold in English departments throughout the country. While he became proficient in that approach for his final project, he brought a more basic and central concern to his reading of Dostoyevsky, Beckett, Conrad, Kertesz, Lawrence and all the other giants he devoured.

He used their work and their lives to gain insight into the meaning of life itself.

My brother Jon and I talked about how walking with Gary through the streets of Champaign was not only like attending a private literary seminar. It also left us with the distinct impression that many of the characters he was discussing with such precision and gusto were at least as alive to him as we who were standing right next to him.

This is not to say that Gary's head was only in books.

He took enormous interest in and displayed tremendous generosity toward me.

I met him only a couple of times as a child, but maintained increasing contact with him starting in 1987, when I first visited Phyllis and him at the home where they lived for the more than 30 years they were together.

Gary was an invariably engaged conversation partner on the phone and in person. He consistently asked probing questions about what I was reading, what I was working on, what I was thinking about for my next move.

Above all, he inquired about Dunreith and Aidan and emphasized their importance in my life.

At the end of each conversation he thanked me for calling him.

Gary gave me and all those who knew him many gifts.

The gift of hearty laughter and shared company.

The gift of a disciplined mind, an unerring hunt for emotional truth and a compassionate soul.

The gift of an unceasing grit and the ability to identify, hold in front of him and feel life's deeper meaning.

How Gary lived his life and how much he gave are also the source of my relief.

He suffered a lot the last year as the ailments kept multiplying and basic functions like eating and walking became harder and harder.

Gary wanted very much to attend my brother Mike and his bride Annie's wedding in October.

His body just would not let him.

When I called him shortly after returning from the West Coast, he compared himself to Poland, surrounded by three empires, but with its flag flying high.

"The monsters are at the gate," he said. "I'm in closure."

But not in so much closure that he couldn't draw on his prodigious memory to quote Cervantes' Don Quixote and tell me, "The next time we speak, Make haste; tell me all, and let not an atom be left behind in the ink-bottle."

Jon and I went down to Champaign twice after that.

The second time was on Saturday, the day before he died.

Gary's hair had never turned grey, but as he lay in the hospital bed in hospice care, we could tell his ravaged body's final breath was near.

I told him quietly that I loved him, that I appreciated all he had done for me and that it would be over soon.

Yesterday, mercifully, it was.

Farewell, Gary.

I thank you for everything.

I will miss you.

And I love you.

RIP, BECKY SIMPSON

July 31, 2013

Dear friend, activist, inspiration and incessantly loving wife, mother, sister, and Mamaw Becky Simpson died earlier this month at age 77. Here is a letter I wrote to her on the plane to Chile on July 11, the day before she died.

Dearest Becky,

This is a note to thank you for all that you have given to your family, your community, the world and me in your 77 years of life. I can't tell you how much you've meant to me in the nearly quarter-century since we first met in the summer of 1989, when I spent a weekend unloading fruit with Bobby, working on the Couch's home near the post office on Route 421 and attending a Saturday night service that Lydia led.

I am so glad that Beverly May had us work and stay with you that weekend.

As you know, I enjoyed the time so much that I called you a year later when I was unable to find a teaching job to see if I could stay with you.

"We can't pay you," you told me. "But we can put you up and feed you."

I'm tremendously grateful I took you up on your offer.

The months I spent living with the rest of your family and you in the fall of 1990 and the visits I made in the years after were some of the most meaningful of my life for many reasons.

I loved being around all of you and being included in the activities.

I loved traveling to pick up food and clothing with Bobby, trying not to get caught by his asking about what had happened to "that box," yelling "Mountain Dew," hearing him call a state trooper who thought we were running moonshine "Honey," and being in a place whose purpose, as you always said, was not to give a handout, but a helping hand.

I also loved spending time with you.

I treasured hearing the stories you told me about your early life in the holler.

About how your first memory was of your brother Buford dying when he took sick during a big rainstorm and your father didn't want to travel over the mountain because it was too dangerous.

About how, the next two winters, you fixed a cup of coffee and stayed up all night with Old Man Joe Hensley so that you wouldn't let your sister Annie die.

About how you used the poultice with crushed onions on her chest to nurse her back to health.

About how you had no shoes and didn't go to school after third grade.

And about how, when the wealthy neighbor told you that she wasn't in the habit of borrowing or lending the sugar you had asked for, you looked straight at her and told her to give it to you.

I appreciated your telling me about marrying Bobby and living in very humble circumstances, about what it was like for you when the floods came and your boy Ricky died in the car accident, and about how your mother was a snake handler who got bit and didn't suffer at all while Preacher Shorty almost died after his bite.

I was honored by your sharing with me about what happened when the flood came, and how, bad back and all, you still managed to pull the children to safety, about how you lost everything, then began to fight at the state and federal level to have the companies take responsibility for the damage the strip mining did to the land, about how you fought for years before getting $1.25 million awarded to dredge the creek, but weren't allowed to participate in the discussions about what happened to the money.

I remember the time you told me about how you were sitting there crying with Mary Beebe on the side of the road most of the way up the mountain when she said, "You can't come to them and they won't come to you, maybe you can find another way."

That was the moment when the vision came for the Survival Center, when you told Bobby that you'd have a mountain of food, a mountain of clothing and a molehill of money.

All three came true.

I will always remember how you stood up to Sidney Fee when he tried to keep you from seeing your family's grave and the story of when you stared down the people who had trapped Sowhali when he was walking down the holler with a white woman.

You showed me how someone can start with so little in a material sense, but, powered by love and justice and a desire to do good, can help tens of thousands of people.

I remember how you never, ever said No to helping someone in whatever way you could, how you gave and gave and gave, to your children, their spouses, your grandchildren and great-grandchildren, the tens of thousands of people who came from youth and church and family groups from all over the country to learn and help and pray and give.

I'm thankful that I got to see and know and spend time with you in the kitchen, to share a pop and see how, despite pain in your teeth and back and jaw no person should ever endure, you just kept giving.

I'll also remember the lighter moments, like your love of professional wrestling and your relationship with your twin Hiram, who always seemed to have a special place in your heart, and how you'd get dressed up and wear heels and do your nails.

Becky, I'm sorry that I never brought Dunreith and Aidan to you and that we didn't complete the project about your life the way I had hoped.

But I do want you to know that I will continue to tell people about you, about your fearlessness and kindness, your tenderness and exquisite generosity, your knowledge of who you are and where you were from, about the grace and strength and grit with which you lived and the glorious legacy you are leaving behind.

I'm sad that I'll not see you again in person and sorry that you have been suffering with lung cancer. It's a hard way to end what has been such a beautiful life, but at least it gives many of the people who have known and loved and been touched and moved and changed by you a chance to share and reach back out to you.

I am one of them.

I thank you.

I'll miss you.

I love you.

Jeff

RIP, ELZIE WHITTINGTON

Dec. 19, 2011

Elzie "Grandma" Whittington lived a full and productive life.
(Photo courtesy of the Lee/Whittington family)

A lot of times you hear about a funeral being a celebration, but it doesn't feel that way.

With Elzie Whittington, childhood friends Scooter and Teo's grandmother who was always "Grandma" to me, it was truly the case.

The stylish silver hat that lay atop her coffin was just one indicator of the strength, wisdom, courage and compassion she displayed during each of her 95 years before she passed last Sunday.

Born in 1916 as one of 16 children to her parents in Ashland, Mississippi, she first showed her wisdom at an early age by learning how to sew in order to get out of the hot sun, said the pastor who presided over the ceremony. She only showed further wisdom, he added, by accepting Jesus in her heart and basing her life on love.

It was a fruitful one.

After moving to Chicago, she met and married George Whittington in 1935. The couple had five children before he died in 1953.

Grandma didn't blink.

Instead she rolled up her sleeves and continued the hard but rewarding work of raising her children to be decent, contributory people.

She succeeded, too, as the first row at A.A. Rayner's filled with smartly-dressed children, grandchildren and other relatives attested.

Grandma didn't just get by though.

She brought all kinds of loving touches to her family, cooking memorably delicious meals, sewing clothes and cutting family members' hair in the latest styles.

The family reciprocated the love she gave, as we heard through the series of moving tributes.

Teo's younger cousin, Will Worley, read a letter from Sage, Scooter's daughter who could not attend the funeral because she was taking her final exams.

"Thank you for teaching me that saying 'What' is not polite," Sage wrote at the beginning of her list of sources of gratitude. "Thank you for making me a corsage when it was my time."

Later, Scooter's mother told me that Grandma made each of her granddaughters a corsage for their Sweet 16.

In Sage's case, Grandma was 94 years old when she did the work.

The pastor made the point that the Bible only promises 70 years, so that Grandma had a quarter century of life on God's time.

When I spoke, I mentioned that the pastor may be right, but Grandma never looked more than 60 or 70 years old to me.

I also talked about her sense of humor, remembering how after Scooter's wedding Grandma, Teo, Mrs. Lee, family friend Bev and I were driving along talking about the wedding.

Who wore what.

Who said what.

The usual.

Then we started laughing.

And laughing.

And laughing.

All of us laughed so hard for what felt like 15 minutes that I said, "My smile is starting to hurt."

A twinkle in her eye, Grandma led that charge.

Teo stood after I spoke.

Pain in his eyes, he talked about Bill Withers' song, "Grandma's Hands." It was all right for other people's grandmothers to co-star in the song, he said, but this was Grandma's song.

After the ceremony, Jon and I went to Aunt Linda's house, site of a legendary barbeque on July 4, 2003. We reunited with the family and did what you do after funerals: eat, enjoy each other's company, eat some more and visit some more.

It was precisely the kind of gathering Grandma would have loved, everyone agreed.

The food was bountiful and lovingly prepared.

Fried chicken. Barbequed chicken. Two types of lasagna. Pasta salad. Four types of cake.

I caught up with Scooter.

We swapped notes about the college application process and how we deal with our kids' dating lives. We shared our conviction about how positively our elementary school teachers had impacted us. And we talked about work and love.

Mrs. Lee told me about Grandma's last day, how she told one of her two remaining daughters that she was an Obama woman through and through.

If they were the only two people who voted for him next November, so be it, Grandma said.

Dunreith arrived.

We chatted with Teo and Sylvia, saw their children Julien and Raven, and then needed to return home for dinner with Aidan, who had just flown in after completing his first semester at Tulane.

We passed Scooter on the street outside Aunt Linda's house.

We hugged, said we loved each other and drove to the highway, edified by Grandma's legacy, challenged to live as fully in the time granted to us as she did in hers, and grateful for the unconditional love she gave and that I was one of so many people privileged to receive.

MEMORIAL TRIBUTE TO ZEZETTE LARSEN

Dec. 16, 2010

Zezette Larsen survived the Auschwitz death camp and lived a full and productive life. *(Photo courtesy of Facing History and Ourselves)*

This one hurt a lot.

Close to 100 people gathered into Facing History's library at the old St. Mary's School in Brookline Village Tuesday night to pay tribute to Zezette Larsen, a survivor of Auschwitz, wife, mother and Facing History board member.

I worked as a program associate at Facing History's Boston office from 1997 to 2000. Spending time with survivors like Zezette or Rena Finder, who was on Schindler's List, was one of my favorite parts of the job.

I didn't have many of those times with Zezette, and the ones I did have stayed with me. In 1998 Facing History had a Choosing to Participate exhibit at the Boston Public Library that included portraits of Holocaust rescuers, a section on the 1957 integration of Central High School in Little Rock, Arkansas, and one about Billings, Montana, where residents of all backgrounds bonded together against anti-Semitic acts.

Zezette was one of the docents who helped the students think about and understand their experience.

My dear friend Dave Russell came to the library with his class of middle school students from the McKinley School in Boston's South End during one of the days that Zezette was there.

Dave's students were in their full adolescent and attention deficit disorder glory when they came upon Zezette and me. I gave them a quick explanation about who she was.

"You a survivor?" one of the students asked her bluntly.

"I am a survivor," she answered.

"It was tough?" the boy asked.

"It was tough," she replied, a trace of her French accent and Belgian roots pushing through on the final word.

Groups of children assess new adults much the way dogs meeting for the first time do, sniffing for signs of weakness.

The boy and the other students responded to Zezette's open and honest acknowledgment of the struggles she knew they were having and of her own past suffering during the war. Rather than hassling her, they nodded and went on quietly to look at the exhibit.

"It was tough" was an understatement of enormous proportions.

Zezette rarely shared her wartime experiences with students when I was at Facing History, but they came through in pieces during the tribute event.

Being hidden in a convent until someone betrayed her.

Sent at age 13 to Auschwitz, where she stayed for two years.

Her parents killed.

The anguish stayed with Zezette her entire life and gave her the compassion to which Dave's students responded.

It was also a large part of why people in the room were grieving so openly.

People's grief took the form of tears–Facing History founder and executive director Margot Strom had them streaming down her face, and Zezette's husband Steve Black broke down at a number of points -and of people like Facing History Program Director Marc Skvirsky saying, "I don't think I can do this."

Fortunately, he did.

Marc brought Zezette into the room through four video clips filmed over the course of two decades starting in the 1980s.

One excerpt was from 1991, when she returned to the death camp, met Steve, fell in love, and got married. Another was from 2001, when she participated on the Facing History civil rights trip in the southern United States.

The clips showed Zezette age with grace and dignity and allowed us to witness her pain as she struggled to name the indescribable loneliness she felt while standing hour after hour during the appel, or roll call, at Auschwitz.

I was trying to survive for an unknown purpose, she said.

Zezette said she had no friendship or connection to anyone else in the place because she was trying like hell not to be noticed.

Friend, poet and human rights activist Marjorie Agosin, who had interviewed Zezette for a book about Jewish-American women called *Uncertain Travelers* and who had previously written a poem about Zezette, read a new one.

So did several other people.

Karen, a woman whom Zezette mentored, sang and brought French and Belgian chocolates.

Sadness descended over me as I bit into a truffle-filled chocolate, telling myself I was doing it in honor of Zezette. If Zezette was an uncertain traveler, she has arrived at a certain destination that will eventually face us all.

So too was the cumulative toll the year has taken.

My father-in-law Marty and stepmother Diane's deaths, Dunreith's car accident, and Mom's heart and hip struggles are the most major blows we have sustained.

Seeing old friends raised my spirits.

Catching up and looking back over dinner with my friend Tracy at Chef Chow's boosted me, too.

I knew appreciation of Zezette's courage in managing the suffering that lifted but never left would eventually come.

And, at that moment, standing among the group that had come together to honor an elegant, wounded and quintessentially human woman, the sadness crowded out everything else.

AVA AND CRAIG MEET

Aug. 11, 2009

Ava Kadishson Schieber and Craig Townsend meet in person.
(Photo courtesy of Jeff Kelly Lowenstein)

Some experiences stay with you.

Not just for minutes or hours.

But days and even weeks.

Like a heavy meal, they take a long time to digest.

Like a 1000-piece puzzle, they require patience to understand the underlying pattern.

Yesterday's meeting between Ava Kadishson Schieber and Craig Townsend was one such experience.

Ava is a Holocaust survivor born in the former Yugoslavia who made it through the war by pretending that she was deaf and mute for four years.

In 1949 she escaped the clutches of Tito's Communist regime and emigrated to Israel, where she married, had three children and was a renowned set designer for an improvisational theater company.

From her earliest years she has been an artist.

Earlier this decade Northwestern University Press published her book *Soundless Roar*, a collection of stories, poems and drawings that render some of her experiences before, during and after the Second World War.

Among many other things, Ava knows about survival and building a life from scratch.

Enter Craig.

He and I met last year during a project I was working on about children with incarcerated parents. Craig was attending a re-entry summit at which I was reporting.

He gave me his wife's name and his family's telephone number.

I gave him a business card.

About a week later a handwritten letter in tight neat cursive letters arrived.

It was from Craig.

I answered and our correspondence began.

Craig is a recovering drug addict who has been incarcerated before.

His girls are 12 and 14. Each has her own personality and memories of life before and after his first incarceration.

Craig wrote often to them while he was away for close to three years for a crime he committed that he says was driven by his addiction.

He called, too.

I interviewed the daughters last summer, close to a year before his return.

The older daughter said, in essence, "I don't know how I feel about only having a year to figure out how I feel about his coming home."

She and the younger daughter both said they did not read the letters he sent–a point confirmed by their mother, Marjana, who was born in Serbia and came to the country with her parents when she was 5 years old.

But when I visited the three of them a couple of weeks ago, the day before he returned, their voices and their hearts thick with emotion, both girls made it clear that the letters had mattered, that the message of love and connection and fatherhood he had sent had been received, if not read.

During our correspondence I initially sent Craig a copy of a blog post I had written about Ava and her book.

Her wisdom and strength moved him.

Deeply.

At Dunreith's suggestion, I sent him Ava's book.

He devoured it in one sitting and shared its contents with other inmates.

In each of his subsequent letters he extended his good wishes to Ava.

He even promoted Ava above my family, telling me to send her his regards ahead of the ones he conveyed to Dunreith and Aidan.

Craig got out from Vandalia Correctional Center about two weeks ago.

We saw each other for the first time in close to a year about a week after that.

One of the first things he asked about was meeting Ava.

Yesterday, it happened.

Craig and Marjana came together, bringing Ava a dozen yellow roses. He put on a blue polo shirt outside her building on Lake Shore Drive.

They entered.

And greeted each other in Serbian.

And hugged.

And sat.

And talked.

The five of us–Dunreith, Ava, Craig, Marjana and I–spent about three hours together in her living room. Craig and Marjana sat with Ava on her soft white sofa, while Dunreith reclined in a chair and I hopped around taking pictures.

Craig told Ava how remarkable she was and how much inspiration she had given him.

She nodded.

For a while we talked about parenting, about trying to give children the value and limits and love that they need, how the times are harder now than they were for young people coming up, and about how we do our best and hope that they have enough.

Over time, the conversation grew deeper.

Craig and Marjana talked about some of the struggles with his daughters he has had since his return.

Together we named some of the dynamics we thought were at play in the situation.

These ranged from kids' natural inclination to pull away at that age to our having an idea of where and when and how we want them. We discussed the difference in his daughters, their memories of the good times before he was arrested and the bad times after his previous return. We talked about his daughters' fear of the conflict repeating, their desire for connection and their possible mistrust of his calmer, more centered, more patient self.

We said how it's hard but necessary for us both to be big as adults while still sharing our hurts.

"He did not waste his time there," Ava said later.

Marjana talked about the Serbian traditions she wanted to uphold, but the pain she felt at her community's initial rejection of Craig because he was not Serbian and is black.

She talked about bringing her older daughter to the Serbian church in which her mother was active and how the community did not accept the baby.

"There was nothing wrong with you, there was something wrong with how they responded," Ava said, touching the younger woman's knee gently.

Marjana cried.

We talked and talked and made plans next time to go to RoseAngelis, Ava's favorite restaurant and a place where she is treated with adulation bordering on reverence. We will bring our children and spend time together as families.

Eventually, Craig and Marjana left to go to a birthday celebration for her father's 67th birthday.

Craig continues to look for work, to reforge connections with his wife and to try to rebuild his relationship with his daughters.

I wrote after the first time I saw him that I did not know what would happen to him.

I still don't.

But I know what I'm hoping for.

And I know I'm glad that the daughter of Serbian immigrants, her husband who speaks five languages and was just released from prison, my Dunreith and I gathered in the home of a indescribably wise and generous spirit, her artwork and the encyclopedias she read while in hiding all around us.

I do know that the meeting brought together many strands of my life–our family's history of the Holocaust, my sharing my life with Dunreith, my love of being with elders, my belief in social justice, the possibility of redemption, the challenges of parenthood and the bone-deep love for our children–all in one emotion-drenched afternoon.

We shared being with each other and we all knew something meaningful had happened, even if we couldn't pinpoint exactly what.

The experience is still with me and will be for a long time to come.

This I know for sure.

SAD LETTER FROM CRAIG TOWNSEND

June 3, 2010

Craig Townsend and Ava Kadishson Schieber hug in happier times.
(Photo by Jeff Kelly Lowenstein)

Usually getting a personal letter in the mail is a joyous experience, but yesterday's was an exception.

The letter was from Craig Townsend.

The address was Pinckneyville Correctional Center.

I first met Craig close to two years ago, when I was working on a story about children with incarcerated parents.

We spoke briefly and I gave him a business card.

A few days later, his first letter arrived in neat black cursive writing.

It was from Craig.

I answered and we began a biweekly correspondence.

Through the course of our correspondence our relationship began to change. Craig wrote about his wife and daughters, all of whom I met, and I in turn shared information about Dunreith and Aidan.

We had to navigate boundaries.

Understandably, Craig took my openness to mean that we were becoming friends, said so and asked me to help him find work. In declining, I wrote that I was still operating within the framework of him as a source–a statement that took him aback for a while.

Nevertheless, we moved forward.

Highly intelligent, Craig is a voracious reader who speaks five languages. In addition to my letters, I started sending him copies of *The Chicago Reporter* and printouts from this blog.

One of the posts was about our dear friend Ava Kadishson Schieber, a Holocaust survivor who, like Craig's wife, comes from the former Yugoslavia. Ava survived during the war by pretending for four years to be deaf and mute, and later wrote *Soundless Roar* about her wartime experience.

Craig was enthralled by Ava's story. At Dunreith's suggestion, I sent him a copy of the book.

He devoured it and started asking about Ava in each letter he wrote.

Craig got out of prison last summer.

Last July I wrote about hanging out with him as he started to piece his life together.

In August, Dunreith, his wife Marjana, Craig and I spent the afternoon at Ava's apartment. At the end of a post about the time, I wrote:

Eventually, Craig and Marjana left to go to a birthday celebration for her father's 67th birthday.

Craig continues to look for work, to reforge connections with his wife and to try to rebuild his relationship with his daughters.

I wrote after the first time I saw him that I did not know what would happen to him.

I still don't.

But I know what I'm hoping for.

And I know I'm glad that the daughter of Serbian immigrants, her husband who speaks five languages and was just released from prison, my Dunreith and

I gathered in the home of a indescribably wise and generous spirit, her artwork and the encyclopedias she read while in hiding all around us.

I do know that the meeting brought together many strands of my life–our family's history of the Holocaust, my sharing my life with Dunreith, my love of being with elders, my belief in social justice, the possibility of redemption, the challenges of parenthood and the bone deep love for our children-all in one emotion-drenched afternoon.

We shared being with each other and we all knew something meaningful had happened, even if we couldn't pinpoint exactly what.

The experience is still with me, and will be for a long time to come.

This I know for sure.

The months after that seemed to be going well for Craig.

In September he spoke at a hearing about children with incarcerated parents and was quoted in several area newspapers. He, community organizer Alex Wiesendanger and I served on a panel about breaking the cycle of incarceration sponsored by Roosevelt University's Mansfield Institute.

Beyond that, he was getting more steady work and had saved enough money to buy a van.

But things remained hard with his kids.

He and I didn't talk as regularly after the new year began.

I considered that a positive development.

Then the bad news started coming.

Craig was found in a car in a forest preserve. He had one of his daughter's prescription medications, which police considered a controlled substance.

The police arrested him.

Now he's in prison.

For a year.

In yesterday's letter, Craig asked for copies of the *Reporter* and printouts from my blog. He asked me to mail Ava a separate letter he had written to her.

And he also wrote, "You opened your life to me to some degree and I became more than a story to you."

More than a story.

Being a reporter is a privilege and an honor, and one that comes with responsibility. People opening their lives is not something I take lightly. Once Craig got out, I no longer considered him a source.

I have not sorted through the range of emotions swirling through me since I received the letter. I still do not know what will happen with Craig and his family.

But I do know that parenting adolescents is a very hard to thing to do under the best of circumstances.

I do know that shared experiences do matter, even if they don't change life outcomes.

I do know that I'm grateful that I've met Craig and am still hoping that he and his family find happier and more peaceful times.

And I do know that tomorrow I'll write him another letter.

THE EMPTY NESTER CHRONICLES, PART I: DROP OFF AT TULANE

Aug. 29, 2011

Aidan stands in front of a sculpture class project at Tulane University.
(Photo by Dunreith Kelly Lowenstein)

Left with him. Came back without him.

That was the main objective of our 941-mile journey there and back to the Crescent City, where Aidan had his first day of classes as a college student at Tulane University today.

We accomplished it with remarkably little drama, no tears and a series of smiling hugs.

We packed up the fire-red Jeep Cherokee the night before departure – a process that left our hallway/dining room more than messy and the back of the Cherokee filled with more stuff than Dunreith said she and her brothers combined took to their colleges.

Illinois gets rural fast outside of Chicago, and the miles and miles of cornstalks and green farms came into focus shortly after we got onto Route 55 outside of Chicago.

We arrived at our friends Michelle and Glenn's place in Memphis shortly before evening and headed over to Central Barbeque for a full slab of wet ribs and pork nachos, the first I had ever eaten.

After having slept most of the day in the car, Aidan was a tad dismayed to realize that New Orleans was nearly 400 miles away from Memphis, rather than the 100 or so he had anticipated.

This meant that we would have to get on the road by 4:00 a.m. in order to arrive at his dorm by 10:00 a.m.

Dunreith and I let him know that our purpose was to get him there when he wanted. Although the ribs, nachos, beer and wine sloshing around in my stomach meant that I got even less sleep than the time I was in bed, we all did our parts and got rolling at the designated time.

The New Orleans humidity smacked us in the face as we pulled into campus just after 10:00 a.m. and were directed to Sharp Hall, Aidan's dorm.

We unloaded the Cherokee's contents. In an arrangement that echoed Noah's ark, he had two large suitcases, two travel suitcases and two gym bags, one green and one blue. Green-shirted orientation volunteers instantly toted them upstairs to the fourth floor.

This was just the beginning of Tulane's version of Southern hospitality. Students gave directions to lost parents like Dunreith and me when asked without a hint of imposition and held the doors open for us to pass through them.

Aidan set right to work getting his room in order. In what was not quite as much of a shocker as the end of *The Crying Game*, he got everything into the appointed space. His printer, computer, toiletries, linens, clothes and books all fit onto his side of the linoleum-covered floor. In no time at all, in fact, Aidan's side looked as if he had been living there for months. The suitcases were in the hallway, ready to be returned to Evanston.

Dunreith and I set off for the French Quarter, where we stayed at the Iberville, a Ritz-Carlton affiliated hotel with Ramada-like prices, thanks to a Tulane parent discount.

Aidan took the St. Charles street car line over to meet us for dinner, and we headed to Felix's Oyster Bar, one of several restaurants in the Quarter that Dunreith's brother Josh had recommended to us. The grilled oysters were soaked in garlic and a gruyere-tasting cheese. Although they may have succeeded in closing my heart's arteries, they also provided plenty of pleasure along the way, as did the bayou sampler of crawfish etouffee, jambalaya and gumbo.

The three of us took the St. Charles trolley line through the Garden District back to Tulane. The breeze that came through the windows and cooled us as we sat on the wooden seats was a welcome relief from the thick heat.

Dunreith and I walked most of the way back to the Quarter, passing under the hundreds, if not thousands, of beads that hung from telephone wires, nearby trees and trolley wires, vestiges of last year's Mardi Gras festivities glinting in the moon and street light.

The Quarter was in full weekend swing, the sounds of street musicians on Bourbon Street mingling with the smell of sweet alcoholic drinks and vomit from those who had enjoyed the Big Easy too much.

The goodbye that we all knew was coming hung over the next day like a rain cloud. It threatened to cover us as we had an unexpected lunch with Aidan after attending a Business School Orientation meeting for parents and purchasing some last-minute computer supplies before heading back to his dorm with the 10 reams of paper we had bought at Office Depot earlier in the morning.

Yet somehow it never burst.

Aidan, who had seemed understandably nervous on the ride south, smiled as he put his hands on his hips before reaching out to Dunreith and hugging her.

I handed him a letter I had written and placed in an Iberville envelope.

"I should have seen that coming," he said before we hugged, too.

We told him we were proud of him and hugged a couple more times before he walked toward the dorm after telling us not to call him until today.

And so, 48 years after a King shared his dream with the nation and the day before the six-year anniversary of an epic hurricane lashed the mouth of the Mississippi with biblical fury, we watched our son walk away from the car that had delivered him to his college and the site of the beginning of his adult life.

I had expected sadness and tears, but, somehow, seeing him settled in, happy to meet new students and ready to dive into the adventures ahead left me feeling uplifted, light even, and present.

Dunreith and I muddled around the directions to get off campus and onto the detour that would take us around the closed I-10 West and back to our home in Evanston.

Our life as empty nesters had begun.

MARATHON MEMORIES AND TODAY'S HORROR

April 15, 2013

Many of my favorite memories ever involve the Boston Marathon.

As a kid growing up in Brookline, I'd walk with my mother to Coolidge Corner and Mile 24.

I thrilled to see the top runners zip by, their strides as free and easy as if they were out for a brisk jog.

I admired the grit of the wheelchair racers who would zoom through just two miles from the finish line.

Seeing Boston legend Johnny Kelley finish his 50th marathon remains a treasured experience.

So, too, does being a witness to the sheer determination of the sea of runners who streamed by in the minutes and hours after the leaders, their strides shortened, their shoulders hunched and their eyes squinting with the pain caused by what they were asking–no, demanding–that their bodies do.

When I was in seventh grade, Joe Santino, our Science teacher, ran Boston for the first time.

Bearded and stocky, with curly hair and thick thighs, he went out too hard and paid the price on Boston's fabled Heartbreak Hill.

But he still finished in a very respectable time of 3:25.

I ran nearly every day of seventh grade. Through Mr. Santino's example, I hatched a goal of someday running Boston myself.

It took me a decade and three training efforts, but I did it.

I ran the race in honor of Dr. D'Angelo, my best friend's father who had died of chronic leukemia just two weeks earlier.

I wore a t-shirt with an image of Dr. D. next to Hank Williams and had told Mrs. D., his widow, that I might pass by Star Market on the corner of Beacon and Tappan Streets around 3:00 p.m.

Like Mr. Santino, I had been too enthusiastic and started walking and running at 20 miles.

Nevertheless, it was almost exactly 3:00 p.m. when I got to Star Market.

Mrs. D'Angelo was there, standing on a wall against the overcast sky. She gave me a silent and gentle wave as I passed.

I almost started crying.

I saw my best friend's brother Gus in the crowd as I rounded the corner and headed for the finish line.

While I could not remember not running when I got there, I vividly remember the feeling of crossing the line and knowing that I had completed a goal that had seemed unattainable for a full 10 years.

Eleven years later, I did it again.

This time, I ran in honor of Paul Tamburello, my fourth grade teacher, mentor and friend who had contracted a non-fatal version of ALS, or Lou Gehrig's Disease.

My brother Mike jumped out of the crowd at Mile 22 on Commonwealth Ave. and guided me home the final four miles.

As opposed to the first time, I had trained more and paced myself better.

This combination allowed me to sprint the final 50 yards and reach the finish line, hearing Mike's cheering voice behind me as I thrust my fist in the air and started yelling.

In addition to my feelings of triumph and vindication, the marathon has always meant so much to me because it's been a shared event. Crowds three, four and five people deep line the course from the very first steps in Hopkinton to the final stride in Copley Square, cheering, celebrating and enjoying the festive atmosphere.

It's a deep part of what makes us Bostonians, a fundamental piece of the fabric of the city and entire New England region.

It's one of the best parts of us, too, the piece that accepts champions from Kenya and Ethiopia and Germany as openly as from other parts of the United States. ("Boston Billy" Rodgers always had a special place in the city's heart.)

We rooted as vigorously for women in wheelchairs as the able-bodied male runners, understanding, in the words of three-time runner up Juma Ikangaa, that everyone is a winner on Marathon Day.

Which is why today's fatal explosions and the gruesome carnage with accompanying heart wrenching details about children and adults killed and maimed are so horribly disturbing.

I talked to Mom tonight.

She said that she was watching the race on television and had even been feeling a little badly that she hadn't again gone to Coolidge Corner, even though the crowds can be too much for her.

Then the explosions happened.

Mom said she's never heard the sound of so many ambulances blaring as they dashed, one by one, by her house on the way to nearby hospitals.

I know that we are now experiencing what has already come to so many other communities.

I also understand that the death toll could have been a lot worse.

But that unfortunate solidarity and grim knowledge of what could have been are scarce comfort to those who have lost loved ones today or for a region that is again forced to confront the lengths to which some twisted individuals will go to destroy life and defile what previously had been sacred ground.

Whoever did this will not succeed, but today marks a profoundly painful shattering of what has been in place and strengthened for generations.

WHAT DO YOU DO WITH YOUR BROKENNESS?

Dec. 17, 2012

Father Michael Lapsley offers closing remarks
at the Engaging the Other conference.
(Photo by Jeff Kelly Lowenstein)

What do you do with your brokenness?

Father Michael Lapsley has had to answer that question since an April morning in 1990.

That's when the New Zealand-born priest and African National Congress member opened a letter bomb sandwiched between a pair of religious magazines at his home in Zimbabwe.

The blast blew off both of Lapsley's arms and cost him the use of his right eye.

Yet, amidst the wreckage of his home and body, there was a glimmer of hope.

Had he opened the letter at a slightly different angle, it would have killed him.

For Olga Macingwane, the question has been posed since 1996.

On that day she and 16 other people were injured by a bomb set by a young right-winger, Stefaans Coetzee, to explode on Christmas Eve in her home community of Worcester, South Africa.

Olga Macingwane prepares to speak at the Engaging the Other Conference.
(Photo by Jeff Kelly Lowenstein)

To this day, she cannot stand for long periods of time.

As a result, she has not held a job.

Worse than that, though, was the loss of her children.

Because the bomb left her physically damaged, Olga was unable to provide the care they needed.

Bowing to reality, she moved them to other people's homes.

For Marguerite Barankitse, the brokenness happened in 1993 during the civil war in Burundi.

Tied and bound naked in front of a church, she was forced to witness the murder of 72 people.

Some of the victims were her family members.

Marguerite Barankitse at the Engaging the Other conference.
(Photo by Jeff Kelly Lowenstein)

Others, she thought, were the seven orphans she had begun to raise after their parents had been murdered.

What do you do with your brokenness?

For Lapsley, the bomb did not slake his thirst for justice and a free, democratic and non-racial South Africa.

He redoubled his religious and political work, returned to his adopted home when permitted to do so and testified before the Truth and Reconciliation Commission.

He told the story of what happened that fateful morning.

If the person came forward and sincerely repented of his actions, of course he would grant the perpetrator forgiveness, he said.

That has not yet happened, but Lapsley's work continues.

He's written a book about his experiences.

He's created the Institute for the Healing of Memories.

And he's expanded his focus from trying to heal South Africa to heal the world.

Lapsley travels more than two-thirds of the year, carrying his message of possibility and hope to whomever he meets

For Olga Macingwane, the brokenness led to silence and anger for more than a dozen years.

In 2009 she heard that Coetzee, after years of reflection and dialogue with imprisoned apartheid killer Eugene de Kock, wanted to meet his victims.

She agreed to meet the bomber, but did not want to speak.

That feeling didn't change in the hours that she rode from Worcester to Pretoria, where Coetzee was being held.

But then he started to talk.

And began to cry.

Olga could see that the man truly repented of his actions and was seeking redemption.

As a Christian, she felt she had to respond.

"When I see you, I see you as my son," she told Coetzee. "I have to forgive you."

They hugged.

Everyone in the room wept.

Marguerite Barankitse negotiated for her life with the killers, one of whom was her cousin.

She said that she would pay them if they released her.

They consented and cut the ropes that bound her.

She was at probably the lowest point imaginable in her life.

Then she heard the orphaned children.

They had hidden in the sacristy.

"We survived so that you could raise us, Mom," they told her.

So she did.

But she didn't stop with them.

Maggie, as she is known, has gone on to raise tens of thousands of orphans from whatever remains of their childhood through to their adulthood.

More than 75 percent of the staff of the organization she founded are orphans she has raised.

What do you do with your brokenness?

People around the world have responded to Lapsley's healing message.

Olga not only gave Coetzee the mother he never had while growing up in an orphanage, she helped save his life.

About 90 percent of the prisoners in Pretoria are black.

They know who the right-wing killers are.

But they also said, "If Olga accepts you, we have to accept you, too."

Maggie has received the Nobel Prize for Children.

More than the international recognition, she has helped the nation write a new page.

A page based on love, new pages that we write for humanity, she said.

In his concluding remarks at the Engaging the Other conference, Father Michael said that the experience of being a victim can lead in two directions.

In his case, as with Olga and Maggie, it lead to becoming a survivor, and, eventually, a victor.

But it can also lead to becoming a victimizer.

He also said that he believes in a day of judgment.

But he added that he does not think that God will ask whether you have ended racism in your country.

But God might ask whether, through your brokenness, you have lived in a way that has made the world more gentle, more kind and more just.

The answer for all of us, he hoped, was Yes.

We know what Maggie, Olga and Father Michael are doing.

What about you?

Section III

OUR CHANGING WORLD

OBAMA'S CHALLENGE, THE USE AND LIMITS OF HISTORY

Jan. 21, 2009

Some of the estimated 1.8 million people who gathered to hear Barack Obama's first inaugural address.
(Photograph by Jon Lowenstein/NOOR)

Now, the work begins.

After a memorable day in which he weathered Chief Justice John Roberts' fumbling of the presidential oath, danced with his wife Michelle to the Etta James tune "At Last" crooned by Grammy Award-winning singer Beyoncé, and attended all 10 inaugural balls, Barack Obama wakes up today as America's first black president.

Yesterday's inauguration was filled with historical symbol and substance.

Obama referred repeatedly to the past in his inaugural address and placed his hand on the same bible that Abraham Lincoln had used close to 150 years earlier.

At different points, Obama invoked immigrants' journeys to America from distant shores, the hardships of slavery and military sacrifice in Concord, Gettysburg and Khe Sanh.

He cited the strength of previous generations in meeting daunting challenges like fascism and communism.

"We are the keepers of this legacy," Obama proclaimed.

Today, he begins, with other elected officials and the public, to work to maintain and advance that noble inheritance.

While doing so, Obama would do well to consider previous presidents' uses of history to positive and negative effect.

The late Harvard professor Richard Neustadt and his colleague, Ernest May, tackle this subject in an illuminating book, *Thinking in Time: The Uses of History for Decision Makers.*

Published in the mid-80s, the work arose out of their classes at the Kennedy School of Government.

During their courses Neustadt and May would examine prior presidents' decisions with an eye toward evaluating how they thought of and used the past to guide their weighty decisions.

It is a decidedly mixed record.

The book begins with the success of the 1962 Cuban Missile Crisis and the saving of Social Security during the 1980s, but also covers a wide range of fiascos from the 1961 Bay of Pigs invasion to the false call in 1976 of an impending flu epidemic to a series of missteps during the Carter Administration.

In many cases, the authors argue, a more thoughtful use of history could have made a difference. They advocate a combination of analysis, the close examination of analogies used to understand the present situation and leaders' placing themselves in the other person's or organization's position.

Neustadt and May suggest that leaders identify what is known, unknown and presumed about the current situation, and then explore the likenesses and differences between previous events and the current moment.

An examination of the presumptions driving the action should be next so as to uncover possibly inaccurate assessments of the situation and likely outcomes that should follow. From there, leaders should try to understand other individuals involved in the situation in part by mapping their life experiences as well as those of the organizations to which they belong–in essence, heeding the Native American injunction not to judge a man until one has walked a mile in his moccasins.

Finally, and perhaps most importantly, leaders should think about their actions in the present as part of an historical stream in which the present bridges from the past to the future.

Franklin Delano Roosevelt had this quality on domestic issues, the authors say, but less so on foreign concerns. Lyndon Baines Johnson had this sensibility on race issues because of his childhood experiences in segregated Texas, but lacked it in the War in Vietnam.

Neustadt and May admit that this method is neither a panacea nor a recipe for transformation–at one point they compare someone who applies it to a baseball player who may raise his average from a mediocre .250 to a slightly better .265–but they do believe it can make a positive difference and help decision makers avoid the Kennedy complaint at the moment of disaster in the Bay of Pigs: "How could I have been so stupid!"

Now, it is Obama's turn to lead us during a seemingly endless and worsening series of challenges.

History will judge his actions, and the closing of his inaugural address suggested that he, at least yesterday, thought in Neustadt and May's time stream.

In this excerpt Obama links his family's journey to the nation's creed and diversity before connecting George Washington's words to a huddled band of soldiers in a desperate hour to what we may someday say to our grandchildren:

"This is the meaning of our liberty and our creed — why men and women and children of every race and every faith can join in celebration across this magnificent Mall, and why a man whose father less than sixty years ago might not have been served at a local restaurant can now stand before you to take a most sacred oath.

So let us mark this day with remembrance, of who we are and how far we have traveled. In the year of America's birth, in the coldest of months, a small band of patriots huddled by dying campfires on the shores of an icy river. The capital was abandoned. The enemy was advancing. The snow was stained with blood. At a moment when the outcome of our revolution was most in doubt, the father of our nation ordered these words be read to the people:

'Let it be told to the future world … that in the depth of winter, when nothing but hope and virtue could survive…that the city and the country, alarmed at one common danger, came forth to meet (it).'

America, in the face of our common dangers, in this winter of our hardship, let us remember these timeless words. With hope and virtue, let us brave once more the icy currents, and endure what storms may come. Let it be said by our children's children that when we were tested we refused to let this journey end, that we did not turn back nor did we falter; and with eyes fixed on the horizon and God's grace upon us, we carried forth that great gift of freedom and delivered it safely to future generations."

Delivered before a throng of more than 1 million people at the Washington Mall, these lofty words will now need to be matched by Obama's individual and our collective action to be given life and meaning.

The work begins today.

JOE WILSON AND STEPHEN KANTROWITZ'S BEN TILLMAN BIOGRAPHY

Sept. 16, 2009

It's been a busy week for U.S. Rep. Joe Wilson.

Since yelling, "You lie!" during President Barack Obama's address about health care reform to a joint session of Congress, the South Carolina Republican has apologized to the president, been formally rebuked by his colleagues in the House and seen his and his Democratic opponent's coffers grow substantially.

Both *New York Times* columnist Maureen Dowd and former President Jimmy Carter have asserted that Wilson's outburst was not only about health care, but also about race.

Dowd speculated that the word "boy" was an unspoken but real element of Wilson's statement, while Carter said that there are many Americans who have not accepted that we have a black president.

My dear friend and University of Wisconsin History Professor Stephen Kantrowitz spent nine years studying white supremacy in South Carolina as it was reflected and actively shaped by Benjamin Ryan Tillman. *Ben Tillman and the Reconstruction of White Supremacy*, his biography of the former Democratic activist, South Carolina governor and U.S. Senator, can help inform a discussion not so much about whether Wilson's statement was racially motivated or not, but on the historic background from which those elements spring.

I have written before about how many converted dissertations bear the mark of an earnest student trying to jump through the hoops necessary to earn a doctorate, a critical credential to enter the academy.

Steve's book is a distinct exception. His first chapter establishes the terrain of slavery and geography in South Carolina in a readable and coherent way.

From there, he turns his considerable powers of analysis to Tillman.

The period that may be most germane for the discussion of Wilson is the post-Reconstruction era, when many vanquished Southerners felt that their entire way of life was under siege. The sentiment was strengthened by the passage of the 14th and 15th Amendments that granted black people equal protection under the law and black men the right to vote, respectively.

During this period and later Tillman used violence to suppress the movement of black people toward their rights, while at the same time vigorously espousing the importance of the rule of law. In a similar and related way, Steve shows how Tillman endorsed an agrarian vision that he traced back to Thomas Jefferson's yeoman farmers, all of whom were white males. While Tillman occasionally paid lip service to equality, he advanced an avowedly white supremacist vision that excluded major sectors of the population. Tillman also had a visceral distrust of the federal government throughout his career.

The connection between Tillman's justification of lynching and Wilson's interruption of Obama may initially seem tenuous–some critics say that anyone who disagrees with the president is immediately called a racist–but a closer look reveals a stronger link.

Tillman's words and actions helped lay the foundation for the violent and oppressive Jim Crow South, the area from which Wilson comes. Wilson's denunciation of Strom Thurmond's biracial daughter, who very possibly was the product of statutory rape, after the senator's death was not a race-neutral statement. Neither is his membership in the Sons of Confederate Veterans.

One can argue that these types of attitudes are a specific function of South Carolina, where political operative Rusty DePass compared an escaped gorilla to "Michelle's relatives."

That would be a superficial and unfortunate misreading. The enthusiastic embrace by conservatives throughout the country of Wilson- "You lie!" t-shirts have already become a hot-selling item–has its roots both in Tillman's deep-seated aversion to the federal government, and, to some degree, in staunch resistance to Obama's right as a black man to hold the nation's highest office.

To be sure, 2009 is not 1868.

Wilson is not Tillman and Obama indeed was elected president by a majority that included millions of white voters.

But his election and governance continues to rouse some of our nation's unvanquished ghosts.

Steve's book helps us understand their origin.

And that's no lie.

AN OPEN LETTER TO PEOPLE PORTRAYING OBAMA AS ADOLF HITLER

Aug. 16, 2009

Just stop it.

You are representing yourself poorly.

You are abusing history.

And you are disrespecting the practice of democratic debate on which this country is based.

Let me be clear about what I bring to this conversation.

I have a personal connection to the Holocaust.

My father was born in Germany and was sent by his parents to England on the Kindertransport shortly before he turned 5 years old.

My Hebrew name is Yosef. I am named for my great-grandfather Joseph Lowenstein, our family's patriarch.

He was murdered in the Auschwitz death camp, along with more than 1 million other people.

In other words, I carry the legacy of the Holocaust with me every day.

But this is not about me or my having a special stake in this topic because of our family's history.

I don't.

Although I can't say for sure, I am confident that I would feel equally strongly about this tactic if my background were different.

This is also not an attempt at censorship.

The images of Obama with a Hitlerian mustache are permissible here under the First Amendment, though they would not be in Germany.

I support your right to express yourself.

I am just asking you to stop this particular form of expression.

There are many reasons behind my request, but I'm going to focus on what to me are the most important.

To begin, Hitler was a genocidal megalomaniac who dismantled democracy in Germany and orchestrated and ordered the killing of millions of people simply because of who they were.

They were Jews.

They were Communists.

They were Jehovah's Witnesses.

They were Roma and Sinti.

They were gay men and lesbians.

Obama is a democratically-elected leader whose campaign elicited unprecedented levels of participation and donations, many from people who had previously been excluded from, or not participated in, the electoral system.

He is proposing to reform a health care system that many say is broken.

To link Obama's proposal and Hitler's actions not only distorts the issue to the point where rational discussion becomes difficult if not impossible, it also demeans the suffering of Hitler's victims.

We are talking about people like Ava Kadishson Schieber, who survived by pretending she was deaf and mute four years on a Serbian farm. Her father and sister were killed for the crime of being Jewish.

We are talking about Elizabeth Dopazo, a Jehovah's Witness whose father refused to sign the Loyalty Oath and was murdered as a result of that decision.

We are also talking about the Polish people who suffered greatly at the hands of Hitler's invading army.

Ironically, Obama himself, as the child of an African father and a white mother, would likely have been sterilized at the least, and killed at worst, had he lived in Hitler's Germany. These were the actions taken by the Nazi government against the children that resulted from relationships between black African soldiers, many of whom were brought in from French colonies after the Treaty of Versailles, and white German women.

Hitler called these children the "Rheinland bastards" and blamed their existence on the Jews.

And let's talk about race.

Hitler had a distinct racial hierarchy into which every group fit.

He laid it all out in *Mein Kampf*, the book he dictated to cellmate Rudolf Hess while serving a stint in prison for attempting to topple the Bavarian government.

At the top, of course, were the blond-haired, blue-eyed Aryans.

Below them were Slavs, who he said were fit to be slaves.

Below them were mixed-race people like Obama.

Then black folks.

Then Jews.

Based on this thinking, Hitler first of all falsely characterized Jews as a race, then used that assertion as the premise for major laws and hundreds of anti-Semitic ordinances.

The Nuremberg Law for the Protection of German Blood and German Honor, passed in 1935, defined who a Jew was.

That law was given life by the measures that forbade Jews from swimming at public beaches, belonging to choral groups, and practicing the professions for which they had studied for years and on which their livelihoods depended.

The ordinances and the law were each designed to take what had been an integrated if vulnerable minority and rip asunder its place in German society.

Obama has no such hateful hierarchy.

While he is unquestionably aware of the significance of his election as the first black president of a country that enshrined the odious practice of slavery three times in its constitution, and while he has delivered major addresses about race, he studiously avoids injecting it into the health care reform debate.

While one could argue that his proposal will help many people of color who are disproportionately among the ranks of the estimated 50 million uninsured Americans, there is no racial supremacy in his world.

Also, please stop accusing Obama on the one hand of wanting to bring in "socialized medicine"–a phrase reform opponents have used since the Truman Administration to stifle change and to raise the specter of Communism–while on the other saying that he embodies totalitarian fascism.

This was a favorite tactics the Nazis used against Jews whom they accused of being simultaneously Bolshevik revolutionaries and capitalist conspirators.

You can see the images for yourself.

This is just one of several ways that your recent tactics resemble those of the man you charge Obama with being.

Nazi propaganda minister Joseph Goebbels talked about how, if you repeat a lie enough times, it becomes true.

Again, I want to be clear.

I'm not accusing you of being a Nazi.

I'm not saying that you believe in a racial hierarchy.

But I am saying that these tactics are dishonest, unproductive, dishonorable and undemocratic.

I am saying that you need to stop them.

Now.

Are there problems with the bill? Could Obama's economic projections be too rosy? Can a legitimate argument be made that the proposal should be defeated?

I'd give a hearty Yes on all accounts.

So, please, join the debate in a way that an actual conversation can happen.

But do it the right way.

Lose the mustache and the fake German accent.

Make an argument.

You might win.

You might not.

But the country will be better for it.

And you might, too.

MATT BAI BREAKS DOWN THE DEMOCRATS' REBUILDING

May 31, 2009

Life is good for the Democratic Party these days.

In firm control of all three branches of government for the first time in more than a generation, the Democrats have seen their ranks swell with the recent defection of U.S. Sen. Arlen Specter of Pennsylvania.

Specter's switch gave the Democrats a near filibuster-proof majority of 59 senators–something that may come in handy during the upcoming nomination process of Sonia Sotomayor, President Barack Obama's nominee to be the next U.S. Supreme Court Justice and the first Latina in the nation's history to serve on the court.

The Democrats have had a string of successes since Obama's inauguration in January, overseeing the passage of a $787 billion stimulus plan, starting to implement a withdrawal time line and process for the war in Iraq and moving both to close the Guantanamo prison camp and repudiating the Bush Administration's interrogation policies that many described as torture.

Meanwhile, the Republicans are struggling. Mightily.

Each week seems to bring new headlines that suggest a party in disarray, with an unclear voice, hierarchy or direction. One week it's Rush Limbaugh saying that Colin Powell is not a true Republican. Another it's Meghan McCain, daughter of the defeated presidential candidate, slamming conservative pundit Ann Coulter.

In this climate, it can be easy to forget that the political scene was completely reversed less than five years ago.

After Bush soundly defeated John Kerry in the November 2004 presidential election, the Democrats seemed to some to be poised on the brink of irrelevance, or, even worse, obscurity. Bush's victory, which gave him the opportunity to appoint two Supreme Court justices, was the seventh by a Republican in the previous 10 presidential contests. Continued majorities in both the House and Senate accompanied his triumph.

New York Times magazine political reporter Matt Bai remembers this dry period in the Democrats' history and traces the party's path back from the political netherlands to reclaiming the House, the Senate and the majority of governorships in *The Argument: Inside the Battle to Remake Democratic Politics*.

The road to political redemption was a twisted one, with many engaging characters and twists along the way.

Bai begins the book with Kerry's crushing, and apparently surprising, defeat in 2004. I had had a strong feeling about the race's outcome from the point that Kerry did not respond forcefully to the Swift Boat attacks in August and thus I did not share the surprise of some of Bai's sources. If anything, Kerry's lack of response reminded me strongly of Michael Dukakis' failure to counter the Lee Atwater-conceived Willie Horton ads that had such a devastating effect on his candidacy.

From the loss, Bai moves to explore the different levels of change in party operation and vision that Democratic strategists and members felt were necessary. Democracy Alliance founder Rob Stein is shown as playing a key role in raising party awareness about the degree of organization the Republicans had fostered, thereby helping people understand what Democrats confronted.

Bai spends a lot of time in the book talking about the ascending role of technology–a development that led to the surprisingly successful candidacy of Howard Dean and his later selection as party chairman, the emerging power of organizations like Eli Pariser's MoveOn.org and the potency of bloggers like Markos Zuniga, creator of the wildly popular DailyKos.

Technology also is a lens through which one sees some of the major conflicts between, on the one hand, the 1990s Clinton-era establishment, which modernized and moved the party toward the political center and fashioned two presidential victories by traditional methods of fundraising and politicking, and, on the other hand, the more progressive and technologically-oriented new guard embodied by Zuniga and Pariser.

The resulting conflicts are often messy.

Bai describes one party gathering where the former president lost his temper when questioned about his wife Hillary's vote to go to war in Iraq and proceeded to rant about all kinds of right-leaning policies and directions he said were ascribed to him. Bai also shows the ongoing and occasionally public struggles between current White House majordomo Rahm Emanuel and the then-party chairman about Dean's 50-state strategy–an approach which Emanuel felt diverted valuable resources from battleground states.

In the end, the Democrats swept to victory. Each of the groups and people listed above and a host of others could claim some share of the triumph, if not the spoils.

The inside argument about remaking Democratic politics is less clearly answered. Bai ends the book with a lion in winter-like address from former New York Governor Mario Cuomo, who reminds the exultant Democrats that, despite their smashing electoral victories, they still "have no big idea."

The Argument has a number of the strengths and weaknesses that characterize much of Bai's work that appears in *The New York Times* magazine. His intelligence, writing skills and thorough reporting are apparent throughout the work; and yet one often leaves his pieces, and, in this case, the book, feeling like she has not learned much new or different.

The Democrats' need to articulate a vision greater than "We are not the Republicans" has been known for a long time, for example. So, too, has the Republicans' superior ground level organizational capacity, forged during the late-70s and 80s by people like Richard Viguerie, strategist Grover Norquist and strengthened in the 90s by Christian Coalition leader Ralph Reed. Bai's explanation of the rise of blogging is engaging but not particularly informative to the tens of millions of people who have clicked onto DailyKos during the past decade.

Bai does not explore the mixed legacy of the Clinton presidency as fully as he could. Ned Lamont's primary victory over Joe Lieberman, which Bai seems to herald as the triumph of the new way, seems a bit hollow, given Lieberman's ultimate victory.

One gets the sense while reading *The Argument* that Bai is writing for those people who were among Rob Stein's target audience–Democrats who did not get why their party was being consistently clobbered in elections, yet did not think that drastic action or rethinking needed to be taken to stop the slide.

Which brings us back to Obama and the Democrats' current strong position.

Obama appears in *The Argument* as a skilled writer who unsurprisingly adopts a both/and position toward traditional party stalwarts and the emerging online progressive movement. He contributes a spirited articulation of his position in a lengthy blog post which urges people not to demonize Republicans, affirms the establishment's importance and uses available technology to share his views.

Written during the throes of Obama and Clinton's fight for the Democratic nomination, the afterword includes the following somewhat prescient thought:

"Should Obama win the nomination, though, and perhaps even the White House, he will face a choice where the powerful progressives in his party are concerned: whether to attempt, through the power of his personality and argument, to lead the new movement away from the limited politics of hostility and toward some modern vision of liberalism, or whether to become, like so many political leaders before him, a reflection of the movement he inherits. If Obama can't change the trajectory of the new progressive movement, then the movement will very likely change him."

Obama has not been president long enough to definitively answer the questions Bai or Cuomo pose The answers may go a long way toward predicting whether his victory is a blip on the screen of Republican dominance or augurs a new era in liberal thinking.

For posing those queries and providing an enjoyable read along the way, Bai deserves credit, even if *The Argument* does have flaws.

OBAMA'S NEW RUSSIAN RELATIONSHIP, CHESS AND THE COLD WAR

March 5, 2009

Among the dizzying array of issues President Barack Obama is tackling these days–the economy, health care, abortion rights, the cessation of torture and education are only some of the most prominent–one that has gotten less attention than many is the United States' involvement with Russia.

Obama has set out to "reboot" America's relationship with its former Cold War adversary.

That effort appeared to take a major step forward earlier this week when he seemed to signal a potential exchange in which, according to the *Associated Press*, the United States would forgo an anti-missile system in Eastern Europe in exchange for Moscow's using its influence with the nettlesome nation of Iran and its burgeoning nuclear ambitions.

Such a move could mark a major advance in relations between the two countries, and could even augur a new era of cooperation between two of the world's most powerful nations.

It has not always been that way.

While the story of the Cold War between the United States and the former Soviet Union has been often, if not exhaustively, told, *Standpoint* editor-in-chief Daniel Johnson recounts it through an unusual lens: the game of chess.

White King and Red Queen: How the Cold War Was Fought on the Chessboard is a gripping book that combines the history of the game waged on 64 black and white squares, the conflict between the United States and the Soviet Union, and the convergences between these two histories during the latter part of the 20th century.

Heartfelt thanks to dear friend Evan Kaplan for supplying me with the book.

White King and Red Queen starts with a brief history of the game of chess before moving into Russia and the former Soviet Union. Johnson shows how the game has resonated in literature, providing an extended analysis of Vladimir Nabokov's novel *The Luzhin Defense*, for instance. Johnson explains how players' experiences have reflected and in a small way shaped the intersection between the game, the passions it evoked, and the gradual suffocating of freedom and relentless bending of individual will to the power of the state that was so characteristic of the former Soviet regime.

In some cases, the knowledge of chess served as a defense against the regime's advances. Dissident Natan Sharansky used his skill to foil his captors' plans to break his will.

Johnson describes effectively how the Soviet Union, through its system of tireless training, dominated the world chess scene essentially unchallenged for a quarter century starting in 1948.

The United States joins the battle later in the century and about a third of the way through the book. The primary warrior for the nation was the brilliant, eccentric and deranged Bobby Fischer, who battled and defeated world champion Boris Spassky in an epic contest in Reykjavik, Iceland in 1972.

Similar to the United States Olympic hockey team victory at Lake Placid eight years later, the contest occurred at a time of serious, but not imminent, threat, and against a backdrop in which a sporting contest between individuals and teams took on far greater geopolitical significance.

Fischer's triumph over Spassky marked the apex of American prowess in the game during the twentieth century, but is far from the end of the book. Johnson has fascinating chapters about the battles between the dissident Victor Korchnoi and the system-supported Anatoly Karpov as well as the struggles waged during the mid- to late-80s between Karpov and Garry Kasparov.

Johnson traces the Soviet system's gradual opening and failing strength under Mikhail Gorbachev and Kasparov's move from opponent to revolutionary after learning about unpunished atrocities in his native Baku in 1990. He also notes, ironically, how the Soviet Union's fall served to strip chess of some of its most compelling matchups. As a result, the game has seen a decrease in international interest and attention. (Kasparov's matches against the computer Deep Blue are the one notable exception.)

The book has many positive aspects. A former literary editor for the *London Times*, Johnson skillfully interweaves historical information, a clear passion for and appreciation of chess and many literary references to tell a highly engaging tale.

It's a tale with an argument.

His feet firmly planted in the conservative camp, Johnson argues that the Soviet's values of repression of individual expression and creativity served to doom it–a defeat that was foreshadowed in Fischer's 1972 victory and that saw its culmination in Kasparov's victories over Karpov during the regime's waning years.

"The Kasparov-Karpov duel was the climax of the story of chess and the Cold War," Johnson writes. "That story is also a hitherto untold chapter in the history of liberty."

Perhaps.

Johnson does an excellent job describing and evoking the atmosphere of terror, dread and intrigue that characterized so much of the Soviet Union's history–a famous phone conversation between Joseph Stalin and author Boris Pasternak is absolutely chilling–but does less well with talking about the American end of the contest.

To be fair to Johnson, this probably has more to do with America's comparatively small influence on the game's history than shortcomings on his part. Still, the point remains that the intersection between chess and politics, societal values and the battles waged between them, is more effectively made on the Soviet than the American side.

This does not detract from a fine work though.

In addition to the assets listed above, *White King and Red Queen* also contains interesting chapters about the rise of computers that play against and handily beat the world's top humans as well as one about the role Jewish players have had in the game's history.

In short, *White King and Red Queen* is a captivating look at the game that people have fallen passionately in love with since its inception and the way the game influenced global struggle during one of the past century's most significant contests of countries, ideologies and ways of life.

BLACK HISTORY MONTH: MARY PATTILLO'S BLACK ON THE BLOCK

Feb. 2, 2009

Mary Pattillo's "Black on the Block" is an engaging read.
(Photo courtesy of Mary Pattillo)

Happy Black History Month!

I'm back after a three-day hiatus during which Dunreith and I had a terrific time in Northern California.

Here's my plan.

In honor of Black History Month, founded by Carter G. Woodson in the late 1920s, I am going to write this month about books that deal with black history.

Today, the work is Northwestern University professor Mary Pattillo's book, *Black on the Block: The Politics of Race and Class in the City*.

Full disclosure: Pattillo has written a letter in support of *The Chicago Reporter*, the magazine for which I work.

Pattillo's first book, *Black Picket Fences: Privilege and Peril Among the Black Middle Class*, dealt with urban, middle-class black communities. She devotes her second work to an analysis of the composition and changes in the North Kenwood/Oakland community on Chicago's South Side.

A central focus of *Black in the Block* for Pattillo is the intra-class interactions between poor and middle-class black people within the community. The title of her second chapter, "The Truly Disadvantaged Meets the Black Bourgeoisie," pays homage to works by scholars E. Franklin Frazier and William Julius Wilson, who taught her during graduate school at the University of Chicago.

Pattillo writes in the introduction that instead of a monolithic block of people, the black community is made of a number of groups that often have fractious discussions:

Disputes between black residents who have professional jobs and those with no jobs, between black families who have been in the neighborhood for generations and those who moved in last year, and between blacks who don fraternity colors and those who sport gang colors, are simultaneously debates about what it means to be black. Choosing participation over abdication and involvement over withdrawal, even and especially when the debates get heated and sometimes vicious, is what constitutes the black community.

In chapters about schools, public housing, and crime, Pattillo shows how these conversations and debates play out. In each chapter, she demonstrates through the often animated conversations and judgments that sharing physical space is not synonymous with sharing a community. Her description of middle class residents' reactions to poorer folks barbecuing in public spaces is particularly well done, for example.

Beyond these specific issues, Pattillo cloaks her analysis in the history of the neighborhood and city. She traces how the neighborhood experienced racial discrimination in housing, a post-World War II heyday, and a period of decline as the manufacturing and industrial economies trailed off and received an infusion of public housing residents.

In addition to developing this context and pushing against the idea of a one-dimensional black community, Pattillo devotes significant amounts of space to the concept and complex reality of the "middlemen"–those middle class black people like aldermen who serve as bridges between the neighborhood and the larger community.

These middlemen and women–Pattillo identifies herself as one such person–are in a tricky position of speaking for the community's need while not denigrating its residents; of being able to bring in, but not single-handedly supply, resources to the neighborhood; and of helping to improve, but also possibly displace, long-term residents.

Pattillo's honesty in describing her own situation in the community and discussion of the middleman are just two of the book's many strengths. Her first chapter, in which she recapitulates the history of her home in the neighborhood that she purchased in 1998, is fascinating, well-researched and innovative.

Through exploring the story of one home, on one block in one community, Pattillo uncovers the city, and, on some level, the nation's uneasy and complicated racial history. It's a past that is replete with racial restrictive covenants, crime drama and racial transition.

This type of storytelling marks a departure from Pattillo's first work, which was converted from her dissertation, and is testament to her intelligence and creativity.

Pattillo demonstrates throughout the book an impressive ability to listen without judgment and with insight – a skill that one sees through the resident conversations and profiles that populate the work. In consecutive chapters she also exhibits her capacity for scholarly restraint by depicting fairly the arguments for and against expanding the number of public housing units in the community.

Chicagophiles and those interested in getting a bead on some of President Obama's top advisers and cabinet ministers will enjoy reading about Valerie Jarrett, Secretary of Education Arne Duncan and John W. Rogers, Jr., in whose offices at Ariel Investments much of the Obama transition was planned.

Pattillo's accomplishments are made even more impressive when one considers the number of scholarly and literary works that have covered the city's South Side before, let alone factoring in the quality of some of those books. Some have said that the South Side is the most-studied area in the world. Luminaries like Wilson, famed novelist Richard Wright, and legendary authors St. Clair Drake and Horace Cayton have all written seminal and enduring works about the community.

To find anything new to say about this area is impressive by itself. To forge a new argument and an innovative way of presenting it is remarkable.

Black on the Block has minor flaws. For example, Pattillo's discussion of middlemen in other cultures is so brief as to be not particularly helpful and she could do more to expand her discussion of Chicago to other American cities. These blemishes only underscore the quality of this thoughtfully-conceived, meticulously documented and skillfully argued work. At a time of national openness about racial issues, *Black on the Block* is a valuable and textured contribution to those conversations.

LINCOLN, KING AND OBAMA'S SECOND INAUGURATION

Jan. 19, 2013

On Sunday, for the second and final time, Barack Hussein Obama will be sworn in as President of the United States by Chief Justice John Roberts.

It will be a moment drenched in historical significance.

In November Obama defeated Republican opponent Mitt Romney, the former governor of Massachusetts, to gain reelection to the nation's highest political office.

America again chose the son of a black Kenyan father and a white American mother to lead it.

For many, Obama's victory was further proof of the progress the country has made in the 150 years since Abraham Lincoln, another lanky lawyer from Illinois, advanced the abolition of slavery and the Congress passed the 13th Amendment.

This August will also mark 50 years since Dr. Martin Luther King, Jr., standing in front of the memorial created in honor of the slain 16th president, spoke without notes in a 15-minute address that instantly and permanently entered the annals of American oratory.

King's speech in front of an estimated 250,000 people has become most well-known in the ensuring decades for its description of his dream that the sons of former slaves and slave owners would eat together at the table of brotherhood, and for his vision that his children would grow up to live in a country in which they would be judged by the content of their character, not the color of their skin.

But the substance of the speech before the articulation of King's dream was that he and all the other marchers had come to urge the nation to make good on its promises.

In his opening paragraphs, King gave a rhetorical tip of the hat to Lincoln's remarks at Gettysburg, perhaps his greatest address, before launching into the guts of his message:

Five score years ago, a great American, in whose symbolic shadow we stand today, signed the Emancipation Proclamation. This momentous decree came as a great beacon light of hope to millions of Negro slaves who had been seared in the flames of withering injustice. It came as a joyous daybreak to end the long night of their captivity.

But one hundred years later, the Negro still is not free. One hundred years later, the life of the Negro is still sadly crippled by the manacles of segregation and the chains of discrimination. One hundred years later, the Negro lives on a lonely island of poverty in the midst of a vast ocean of material prosperity. One hundred years later, the Negro is still languishing in the corners of American society and finds himself an exile in his own land. So we have come here today to dramatize a shameful condition.

In a sense we have come to our nation's capital to cash a check. When the architects of our republic wrote the magnificent words of the Constitution and the Declaration of Independence, they were signing a promissory note to which every American was to fall heir. This note was a promise that all men, yes, black men as well as white men, would be guaranteed the unalienable rights of life, liberty, and the pursuit of happiness.

For those familiar with King's rhetoric, these opening paragraphs bring out one of the major thrusts of his arguments made in his earliest days as an impromptu leader of the Montgomery Bus Boycott that catapulted him to national prominence through to his final campaign in Memphis: America had not fulfilled its lofty promises.

The people who were protesting were urging the nation to be true to its creed.

"And we are not wrong; we are not wrong in what we are doing," King declared at one of the first meetings of the Montgomery Improvement Association that was convened after Rosa Parks' arrest. "(Well) If we are wrong, the Supreme Court of this nation is wrong. (Yes sir) [applause] If we are wrong, the Constitution of the United States is wrong."

Obama will bring Lincoln and King together during his oath of office by placing his hand on two bibles stacked on top of each other.

The holy book he used four years ago belonged to Lincoln.

The other is a traveling bible owned by Dr. King.

It is important to appreciate just how far the nation, pushed by the protests of thousands of ordinary Americans, has come since King's memorable address.

Indeed, it can be tempting at this moment to look at Obama's victories–something that literally seemed inconceivable less than 20 years ago–and conclude that America has truly become a post-racial society.

That would be a mistake.

While there has been great progress, so, too, is there much work to do before the nation can say that the promises of democracy have truly been extended to all Americans.

There are more Americans living in poverty than at any time in our nation's history.

Black people continue to be highly overrepresented in America's prisons.

We still live in very segregated communities.

Our children attend unequal schools.

I could go on, and you get the idea.

In his first campaign, Obama offered soaring promises of transformational change that he followed with what many felt was overly cautious and compromising governance.

This summer and fall, he advanced a more measured, less ambitious plan for America. Since November he has shown less willingness to compromise with his implacable opponents and a stronger desire to take on unpopular issues like immigration reform.

The eyes of the nation and the world will be on him on Monday, when the public ceremonies take place.

Mindful of the progress the nation has made and aware of the unfinished business that lies ahead, I will be watching, too.

JACOB HOLDT'S AMERICAN PICTURES

March 27, 2009

Jacob Holdt has shown his multimedia
slideshow about America
for more than 30 years.
(Photo courtesy of Poul Rasmussen)

Headlines about the brutal economy are plastered everywhere these days.

From outrage at multiple bailout recipient AIG's initial decision to award executive bonuses to the monthly accounting of job losses to advice about how to weather the storm, the issue is dominating news coverage and public conversation.

Many people have commented how this recession differs from others both in its severity and in its impact on middle class Americans. Whereas previous downturns had primarily affected people at the bottom of the economic ladder, this shakeout has had much broader consequences for people of all classes.

In the early 1970s, Jacob Holdt, a young Dane with long, flowing brown hair and a braided beard, came to the United States.

During the next five years he hitchhiked across the United States. Living as a self-described vagabond, he stayed wherever he could and sold his blood plasma to take pictures to record his journey.

In all, he spent $40, or $8 per year.

American Pictures, a searing, stimulating and somewhat flawed look at the United States in the mid-70s, is the result.

American Pictures is a complement to the hours-long multi-media show Holdt has presented thousands of times on American campuses. The project combines Holdt's pictures, music from Jimmy Cliff, Aretha Franklin and Holly Near, among others, and his words.

Holdt's essential contention is that, more than a century after the Emancipation Proclamation, America is still a master-slave society, with whites retaining their dominant role and black people still being confined to sub-human conditions.

The images have tremendous power.

Holdt shows the simultaneous suffering of black people and enormous riches of many whites–wealth that in many cases comes as a direct result of black people's labor.

He shows wrenching pictures of black people picking cotton, children with runny noses, junkies shooting up to dull their pain and families living in ramshackle homes.

His interview subjects include a former slave, people who are so poor they eat dirt, southern white racists and Julie Nixon, daughter of former President Richard Nixon.

The book's text is a combination of letter excerpts that accompany the images and essays that advance Holdt's thesis.

He repeatedly has strong words for white liberals who espouse different values than their conservative or more overtly racist counterparts, but who benefit from the system and do nothing substantial to change it.

Despite all the oppression endured by black people, Holdt also shows the resilience, love and tenderness that exist among and between many in the community.

He tries to maintain an openness toward wealthy people and spends time with some of America's most prominent families like the Kennedys and Rockefellers.

While the book and multi-media show are dominated by images of African-Americans, Holdt does have some material about the 1973 struggle by the American Indian Movement at Wounded Knee, which he describes as a partial victory.

American Pictures has multiple strong points.

Like his countryman, Jacob Riis, whose work, *How The Other Half Lives*, brought to light the suffering experienced by many Americans in the late 19th century, Holdt has dedicated his life to witnessing, documenting and sharing with others the lives of America's underclass. His work is underpinned by a profoundly moral vision and, from his life in Denmark, an understanding that socially progressive policies are possible.

The power of his images is undeniable, particularly when seen in conjunction with the music and narration. My brother Jon and I first saw *American Pictures* at Holdt's home in Copenhagen in the summer of 1985, the night before I was returning to the United States from studying in Florence and traveling in Europe.

Flying into New York's Kennedy Airport and seeing black sky caps wait on almost exclusively white passengers gave me an insight into a country in which I had lived, but not fully seen before.

He also questions his own actions and finds himself wanting. Holdt recounts a failed marriage to a black American woman whom he struck during an argument and often questions whether his art is simply another vehicle to exploit an already abused people.

Still, the work has several significant challenges.

Black people are presented as an undifferentiated mass and almost exclusively as victims. While there are scenes of connection and physical intimacy between African Americans–at times one wonders about Holdt's specific purpose in including multiple pictures of naked black women–their number and emotional resonance are dwarfed by the unrelenting misery that he depicts.

There are many black people who are not part of the underclass that Holdt shows, yet a viewer would not know it from watching and listening to his powerful presentation.

Holdt also has an almost completely binary vision of American society. While native peoples are mentioned in the section on Wounded Knee, the country's millions of Latinos, who have outnumbered black people in America for several years, are nowhere to be seen. This absence is striking because Holdt's analysis is predicated on the omission of a major group within American society.

Holdt's relationship to his subjects is another issue to consider. He makes the argument in the book that his outsider status, vagabond philosophy and facial hair make him almost exempt from the racial structures of American society.

Having spent a year in South Africa in the mid-90s, I understand what Holdt means and give him full credit for traveling to the places he did and documenting what he saw. I will also say that I concluded in retrospect that my assumptions of immunity from South Africa's racial dynamics because of my good intentions and willingness to go to places where many white South Africans did not venture seem less convincing than they did at the time.

To be fair, Holdt has expanded his focus beyond the contents of version of the book that I have to work for Third World development. His commitment to the underclass and to public conversation is highly laudable. Even with its significant areas of omission and lack of distinction, *American Pictures* is a valuable contribution toward gaining a fuller understanding of American society.

MADISON PROTESTS NOW AND IN 1967

Feb. 21, 2011

With the nation locked in a seemingly interminable conflict in a faraway land, the eyes of the world were on Madison, Wisconsin this week, where thousands of people descended on the state's capital on Saturday.

The wars in Afghanistan and Iraq were in the background to the protestors, who were contesting what they saw as an effort by Republican Gov. Scott Walker and the Republican-controlled legislature to impose draconian budget cuts and strip public sector employees of their collective bargaining rights.

Dear friend and University of Wisconsin-Madison History professor Steve Kantrowitz told me yesterday that the sidewalks and streets around the capital building were packed with people expressing their opposition in nonviolent and peaceful fashion. Steve's exhilaration crackled across the line as he described the power of being among such a committed, disciplined and joyful crowd.

His children Elliot and Sophie were with him.

While it is unclear how much Sophie will remember of her initial protest, the odds are quite favorable that Elliot, who is approaching 10 years old, will have clear memories of Saturday's sights, sounds and smells.

Of course, this is not the first time that a world spotlight has focused on Madison.

The university where Steve has taught since graduating from Princeton in 1995 was home to some of the most dramatic, early and disturbing confrontations between students registering their outrage at the Vietnam War and area police.

Pulitzer Prize-winning author and Madison native David Maraniss was an 18-year-old freshman at the time. The indelible impression of observing the protests and feeling the sting of tear gas in October 1967 never left him.

Thirty-four years later, he returned with his wife to their hometown to learn more about those events and that time. But Maraniss didn't only focus on the domestic upheaval. Rather he also investigated a bloody battle in Ong Nguyen in which 58 American soldiers were killed.

The simultaneous protest at home and war abroad form the dominant narrative threads of *They Marched Into Sunlight*, Maraniss' impressive and often gripping evocation of a deeply troubled era in the nation's history whose echoes still rebound today.

Thanks to friend and Vietnam veteran Chuck Meyers for lending me the work.

The book draw its title from an inversion of a line from a poem by Bruce Weigl, who wrote about a line of infantrymen marching into a deadly battle. It primarily applies to the soldiers, so many of whom die far before their time.

Maraniss creates vivid portraits of All-American football player and Major Donald "Holly" Holleder as well as of Terry Allen, Jr., the son of a World War II general and the First Lieutenant who led his men to their death while his marriage was crumbling back home. Maraniss also writes about Danny Sikorski, scion of a Polish family who he argues was an archetypal soldier, and blond-haired Jack Schroder, who was studying to be a dental technician and wrote about his concern before the mission.

All served.

All marched.

All were killed.

Yet the youth back in Madison were also walking into a different type of sunlight. Beyond the physical injuries they sustained from the police's brutal conduct and head smashing, many of the students and others in the university community saw their faith in the social compact that prized vigorous debate as the cornerstone of academic life and discourse shattered.

Maraniss focuses his considerable descriptive and reporting powers in these sections of the book on people like Paul Soglin, who eventually becomes mayor of the city, and Jonathan Stielstra, whose cutting of the flag from the Bascom Hall roof set off a manhunt.

The war's architects in the Johnson Administration, the source of soldiers and protestors' discontents, constitute the third thread of Maraniss' story. Johnson and his familiar cast of characters do not appear as often or in as much depth as either side of the war and peace divide. But Maraniss writes enough to convey their sharpening awareness that the war was unwinnable while they continued to prosecute it.

The failure and dishonesty of leaders is a consistent theme in the work. Readers of Jonathan Shay's *Achilles in Vietnam* will remember the rage engendered in Achilles when Agamemnon violates his trust and betrays him by claiming the top prize Achilles had earned. Shay argues in his groundbreaking work that American soldiers in Vietnam had the same experience when their leaders betrayed them.

This is shown most through the behavior of Gen. William Westmoreland, who briskly informs one of the battle's survivors that there was no ambush when that in fact was the case. On a broader level, though, the whole story is an indictment of the series of decisions by political and military leaders that led to seemingly endless carnage on both sides.

They Marched Into Sunlight is not a polemic, however.

Maraniss writes with some sympathy and complexity about Chancellor William Sewell, a liberal sociologist who had been tapped to fill the position and who found himself torn between the law and order and First Amendment positions advocated by both sides of the protest. A young Dick Cheney, who had gotten kicked out of Yale twice and did not serve in the war, makes a number of appearances in the work and does not emerge unscathed, either.

The book ends with the funerals for the soldiers killed in the battle, which took place at almost the same time as the march on the Pentagon that led to Norman Mailer's *The Armies of the Night*.

In the epilogue, Maraniss updates the story by talking about what happened to the characters in the book in the 34 years after the events covered in the work.

This includes a trip to Vietnam, where Clark Welch, one of the American soldiers, meets with a former Viet Cong adversary. A protestor and soldier are bonded through their children, as the son of one of the Madison students marries the daughter of one of the surviving soldiers. Within the same family, people on both sides of the issue find some peace, too.

Familial peace does mean a lot, but obviously does not signify broader social harmony or resolution of the issues that divided the people and their countries.

The events in Madison Saturday, in which Tea Party members also participated, show that the nation, while divided, perhaps has gotten to a place where those in law enforcement or the military are no longer called "pigs" or "baby killers."

This is progress, even as budget cut opponents and public sectors may ultimately lose this battle.

Maraniss' work reminds us of that painful period by focusing on a Midwestern capital that once again may be serving as a bellwether for our country's questions of the day.

I also look forward to reading in 2045 or so the account that a now-Wisconsin freshman, or people like Steve's son Elliot, will write about last weekend's events.

JOHN EDGAR WIDEMAN'S "BROTHERS AND KEEPERS"

Feb. 18, 2009

A drug deal goes bad.

Shots are fired.

One life ends and others are permanently changed.

In the mid-70s, John Edgar Wideman's brother Robby was involved in such an incident.

Brothers and Keepers, a beautiful, searing and haunting book, is the result.

The work opens with Wideman getting the news about the murder from his mother on the telephone. He's in Laramie, Wyoming, thousands of miles from his childhood home in Pittsburgh's Homewood neighborhood. Shortly after, Wideman is visited by his brother Robby and his two partners.

All three are on the lam.

The fugitives spend a night at Wideman's house before continuing their flight from justice, which ends just days after the stop in Wyoming.

The news, of course, is shattering.

Nearly a decade older than Robby, Wideman feels guilt at not having been able to steer his brother in a different direction. He also sees the crumbling of the wall he has built with ambivalence between his original black neighborhood and his adult world of teaching, marrying a white woman, writing and parenting.

Brothers and Keepers is a collaboration between Robby and Wideman in the fullest sense.

After an initial section in which Wideman describes the crime, Robby's flight from justice and the process of bringing his family to visit his brother, Robby's voice enters the work and alternates with his older brother's words.

I wrote recently about *Hoop Roots*, Wideman's paean to basketball and the Homewood neighborhood, and a work that I liked, but did not love.

Brothers and Keepers got me from the opening sentence and furthered its grip on my attention and emotions throughout the work.

One section is filled with tenderness toward Wideman's daughter Jamila, with whom he feels a special bond after her premature birth and desperate fight for life. The depiction of Robby's final conflict with his parents, which begins with Robby's defying his ban on phone use and ends with his wielding a pair of scissors toward his father, is enthralling and drenched with pain. So, too, is Wideman's description of his mother's unending love for her son, which she tries to reconcile with what she sees as the justice system's denial of Robby's humanity.

These sections are rendered with varying sentence length and lots of telling physical detail. But the book's deepest power comes from Wideman and Robby's interactions, Wideman's reflections on their choices and paths, and his explication of the visceral love between brothers.

In addition to being intensely personal, *Brothers and Keepers* is very explicitly about race. At different points, Wideman alludes to Paul Laurence Dunbar's *Mask* and Ralph Ellison's *Invisible Man*. Robby's joining Wideman for a night at his house after the murder puts the elder brother in legal jeopardy. It also shatters the physical and psychic distance Wideman has constructed between his original home and his adult life, and forces him to consider the costs of both.

Succeeding in the white world that began when he attended the University of Pennsylvania has meant, to some degree, an erosion of who Wideman was and where he came from. Yet, for him, staying in Homewood would have meant that he could have continued down the same path on which Robby ended.

Robby emerges as a poignant figure, too.

His vernacular talk takes the reader into his world and shows his emerging sense of responsibility, his spiritual journey through Islam and his efforts to maintain his sanity and hope. Wideman exhibits great skill in showing the contradictory nature of Robby's life. He is most alone when with other people. The tenacity and aggression that led him to participate in the murder are the qualities that allow him to fight for and retain his dignity.

Through Robby's words and Wideman's reflections, we come to understand how Robby's life and choices are similar to those faced by Wideman, figures in Greek stories and all of us.

As the book progresses, too, Wideman faces his own limitations, his own poor choices and comes to a greater acceptance of the path he has forged. This compassion extends toward Robby and other family members.

Brothers and Keepers becomes even more moving when one reflects on the explosion of incarceration that has occurred in the quarter century since its publication. Toward the end of the book, Wideman notes that the number of people who are incarcerated was about 500,000 and growing and that the United States' rate of incarceration was exceeded only by that of South Africa and the then-Soviet Union.

The rate is now the world's highest.

The total is greater than 2 million.

And black men populate our nation's prisons at a rate far higher than their share of the population.

On a more personal note, one of Wideman's sons, Jacob, was later convicted of murder after a fellow camper was found stabbed to death.

This later knowledge suffuses *Brothers and Keepers* with an additional layer of pain, irony, guilt, remorse and hope in the possibility of redemption.

Brothers and Keepers ends with Robby's valedictory speech at a prison graduation and a letter to his older brother. The address contains a plea for meaningful rehabilitation that finishes on a note of gratitude. In the letter, Robby recounts the legal setbacks he has experienced and closes with the affirmation,

"Be cool, bro.

I SHALL ALWAYS PRAY."

The combination of prayer and connection, blended with the injunction from a younger brother to his oldest sibling to keep the faith, is a fitting end to this remarkable book.

REV. HOOD BRINGS TOGETHER PEOPLE WORKING FOR PEACE

Nov. 24 2009

The Rev. Robin Hood looks on as former gang member Derek Brown talks about his efforts to bring peace to the North Lawndale community.
(Photograph by Jeff Kelly Lowenstein)

Violence has claimed the lives of far too many young people in Chicago.

On Saturday morning, the Rev. Robin Hood of Clergy Committed to Community brought together about two dozen people at Pastor John Drummond's New Grace Emmanuel Church in the South Chicago neighborhood to figure out how to stop it.

Most of the people in the pews were black women. Some had children with them, and many wore green t-shirts proclaiming their membership in Mothers Opposed to Violence Everywhere, or MOVE. Four Latino mothers who belong to Mothers for Peace in the Back of the Yards neighborhood sat in a pew in the second row.

The late November morning was sunny and temperate, but the content the speakers discussed was not.

Derek Brown, earlier known as "Shotgun," spoke after Rev. Hood gave introductory comments. A former high-ranking member of the Vice Lords gang, Brown talked about the work he has done with the youth in his native North Lawndale community to reduce the violence that has been so rampant.

"It's easy," said Brown, who has a shaved head, full beard and thick, muscled arms covered with tattoos. "Give them something to do and keep them focused."

One of the somethings Brown has done is start a boxing club. This past week he helped organize a talent show that hundreds of kids attended.

Brown explained that funding thus far has come through grace and his and other young men's visits to businesses in the community.

Lisa Rivera of Mothers for Peace talked about the importance of loving children unconditionally. Her shoulder-length black hair flashing as she spoke, she explained that she has come to realize that condemning her son's behavior may have pushed him to the street corner, where gang members were waiting for him with open arms.

Rivera, whose 20-year-old son has been incarcerated for two years, visits him every week in prison. Her group has held meetings with gang members in the community, and the word is spreading.

James Thindwa spoke last.

The Zimbabwean-born former head of Jobs for Justice acknowledged the importance of taking responsibility for children's actions. But he also talked about the necessity of holding politicians accountable and recognizing the devastating impact job loss has had on black and Latino communities.

"Let's have both conversations," Thindwa said, his voice rising as he spoke about Mayor Daley's 2006 veto of the living wage ordinance that passed the City Council and the $14 billion the United States spends monthly on wars in Iraq and Afghanistan.

Many questions remain.

An elder in a black three-piece suit asked Brown how others who have less street credibility can intervene with the young people in the community.

Brown's answer to "show no fear" did not appear to satisfy him.

Several speakers denounced violence in the community while at the same time appearing to condone hitting children as an acceptable form of discipline.

Some of the statistics speakers mentioned were of questionable accuracy.

But a start was made.

On a clean and quiet street in one of the neighborhoods hardest hit by violence, black and brown people came together to talk, support each other, forge alliances and design solutions.

They spoke from their hearts.

They listened with respect.

And they gave each other strength to continue the fight.

FATHER GREG BOYLE WRITES ABOUT TATTOOS ON THE HEART

July 30, 2011

It's a beautiful thing when words can make you cry.

Father Greg Boyle's *Tattoos on the Heart* did it to me over and over again.

For those who do not know, Boyle is the founder of Homeboy Industries, the nationally-acclaimed project that provides former gang members with all manner of services, from tattoo removal to a job to therapy to legal help.

The book is peppered with vignettes from his quarter century working in Los Angeles' poorest neighborhoods–a period during which he has buried more than 175 gang members killed by rivals.

A skilled raconteur and deft writer with a gift for dialogue and telling detail, Boyle takes the reader through many of the moments that have both wounded and healed during his casting his lot with the poor.

In *Tattoos* we meet former gang members trying to heal from unspeakable child abuse and create a different way for themselves and their children. In one story, for instance, Boyle writes about a young man who gets his first job ever as a rat at Chuck E. Cheese. The suit is hot and uncomfortable and kids poke at him constantly, but the former gang member keeps working because his son will be born in two months and he wants his boy to grow up with a working father.

Homeboy Industries began with a bakery in which the workers had to share space and time with former enemies, including those who killed fellow gang and even family members.

Boyle describes Puppet and Youngster, two such workers between which something so fearsome had passed that they refused to shake each other's hands and worked together in tense silence for six months.

Yet when Puppet was beaten beyond all recognition, Youngster asked Boyle if he could donate some blood to his former adversary.

Many of the stories are soaked through with pain and the undeniable reality that life will end too soon and too young for far too many of these young men and women.

In some cases, the wounds come from and bring home the consequences of their actions.

Boyle tells the story of two brothers who danced around the gang life before joining it. A shooting near their home did not kill them, but claimed the life of their younger brother who had no affiliation instead.

Other former gang members are gunned down in daylight and without provocation. One young man who had worked 20 years to gain a fierce reputation he concluded he did not want was killed while removing graffiti from the community.

These false starts and incomplete efforts at redemption add a deeper level to the suffering so many in the community endure. Boyle writes about the question of success, drawing on the words of others to conclude that it lies not so much in the outcome, but the effort.

Literate and spiritual, *Tattoos* also drops in liturgy with quotes from writers ranging from Buddhist teacher Pema Chodron to poet Mary Oliver to Pierre Teillard de Chardin. These excerpts cast the specific stories Boyle recounts in a larger purpose of seeking to restore all of God's creatures to their intact, beautiful, shame-free selves, and of urging everyone not to segregate themselves from the outcasts among us.

Boyle writes about the early days of his church in Dolores Mission, when he had started to welcome homeless people into the parish. The visitors' smell got to the point when he felt he had to address it.

He asked the parishioners what the church smells like.

"Like feet," an older gentleman answers in a loud voice.

While not denying the answer, Boyle then led his congregation through the process of identifying the source of the odor and the reason for their presence in the church.

He repeated the question.

This time, the answer was different.

"It smells like our commitment to Jesus," one woman answered.

"It smells like roses," said another.

These tender moments of connection and kinship keep Boyle going and provide the backdrop for his description of his work's evolution.

As a younger priest, he drove his bicycle around the housing projects where he worked and lived, intervening in conflicts and even mediating truces between gangs.

In addition to keeping an unsustainable pace that burned him out, he also came to conclude that the negotiations legitimized the gangs.

That process of growth and change continues.

In the time he spent with us on Tuesday, Father Boyle told us that he now feels uncomfortable with the expression he used to champion, "Nothing beats a bullet like a job."

But now he has arrived at the conclusion that he is seeking to help the thousands of young men and women who enter Homeboy Industries' doors transform their identities from where they are to the spouses, parents, workers and contributors they have within them waiting to emerge.

It's a glorious vision that has materialized often enough, and with sufficient joy, humor and connection along the way, for Boyle to conclude that at times he must sit back and soak in his good fortune.

Tattoos on the Heart articulates that vision in a way that provokes outrage at the conditions into which these young people are born, moves the reader to tears at their resilience, heart and all-too-frequent early demises, and inspires us to consider what we can do to make a small but real contribution to this and other causes.

PUSHING THROUGH THE RED STATE/BLUE STATE DICHOTOMY

Jan. 11, 2009

Bill Bishop tackles the issue
of how America came to be
so divided in The Big Sort.
(Photo courtesy of Bill Bishop)

The idea of blue states and red states is a widely, if not universally, accepted concept in American politics.

Every four years pundits and news anchors like Brian Williams–and before him the troika of the late Peter Jennings, Tom Brokaw and Dan Rather–stand in front of maps of the United States, projecting which states will turn Democratic blue or Republican red.

Many have commented about the political and cultural divide between blue states, located on the coasts and in parts of the Midwest, and the red states, which are everywhere else.

Others have contested that notion.

In his 2004 keynote speech at the Democratic National Convention that contributed toward launching him to political superstardom, then-U.S. Senate candidate Barack Obama declared, in one of many memorable phrases:

"The pundits, the pundits like to slice and dice our country into red states and blue States: red states for Republicans, blue States for Democrats. But I've got news for them, too. We worship an awesome God in the blue states, and we don't like federal agents poking around our libraries in the red states.

We coach little league in the blue states and, yes, we've got some gay friends in the red states."

Obama's point was that the blue and red distinctions do not apply to people's lives. Rather than thinking in these terms, Obama said, we would be better served to base our actions on the recognition that there is "a single American family."

Since that speech, Obama has continued to advance that same message of national unity–and has been rewarded handsomely.

The center of a meteoric rise that is without precedent in American history, Obama shattered fund raising records on the way to winning a historic victory November 4 that will culminate in his inauguration just 10 days from today.

As Obama's time to govern approaches, he confronts no end of daunting problems. An economy teetering on the edge of catastrophe, two wars, and conflict in the Middle East possibly sparking a global conflagration top a very long list.

Meeting these challenges will require drawing on the commonality that Obama asserted exists throughout the country.

Obama may find this common ground in shorter supply than he would like, but not for the reasons he articulated in his 2004 keynote speech.

The Big Sort: Why The Clustering of Like-Minded America Is Tearing Us Apart, an intriguing book by journalist and editor Bill Bishop, with heavy research assistance from retired University of Texas at Austin sociology professor Robert Cushing, may hold the key to help Obama and other readers understand that resistance.

Drawing on an engaging blend of election and census data analysis, shoe-leather reporting, psychology and historical interpretation, Bishop argues that millions of Americans have, largely unconsciously, participated during the past 35 years in a national sorting process whereby they live in ever-more homogeneous communities.

The consequences of this sorting have been profound, he says. Bishop maintains that this homogeneity has led to the near disappearance of the political center, a diminished public discourse and an entitled populace who approach democracy as consumers, rather than participants.

The sorting has been driven by a number of factors, one of the most important of which has been the increased mobility in America during the past three decades.

While acknowledging that America has seen massive migrations before–Bishop refers to the Second Great Migration of African Americans to northern urban centers like Chicago and Detroit in the 1950s–the migration from 1970 to 2000 differed from earlier versions because it was selective and based on personal characteristics, rather than broad demographic similarities.

The ability to choose to live in areas where other like-minded people have gathered before, Bishop says, has led to the formation of thousands of polarized communities divided along political, economic and cultural lines.

Bishop cites evidence from national elections to buttress his assertions. His tracing of the decrease of political moderates from 1976 to the middle of this decade is noteworthy, as are the maps which show the growing number of communities where one presidential candidate or another won a victory of at least 20 points over his opponent.

Bishop's book is far from a recitation of statistics.

A fascinating section discusses the boarding houses in Washington, DC, where representatives from each major party stay.

By staying in these houses until Thursday night, when they head back to their districts, these representatives have less contact and dialogue with people from the other party than they did in the past. Bishop argues that this phenomenon is a microcosm of what has happened in the nation as a whole.

These sections and nuggets are among the book's strongest. (His explanation for the reasons that led to the sorting, starting in what he describes as a watershed year of 1965, is more thought-provoking than illuminating.) Bishop employs with success the skills he plied as a projects reporter for the *Austin American-Statesman* with Cushing's data and other fields to point out divisions that have not been identified before.

Bishop's gloom about the democratic implications echo those raised about technology by Office of Information and Regulatory Affairs chief and noted scholar Cass Sunstein in *Republic 2.0*.

As impressive as these attributes are, the book's analysis seems more convincing in explaining the electoral map of 2004, when George W. Bush scored a narrow victory over John Kerry, than Obama's triumph over John McCain in 2008.

Just three states switched political allegiance from the bitterly contested 2000 race between Bush and then Vice President Al Gore to 2004. By contrast, Obama won nine more states and received more than 10 million more votes than Kerry had four years earlier.

The electoral and financial support of a candidate whose central message based on unity and possibility challenges Bishop's argument.

To be fair, winning an election is not the same as debating and forging a collective legislative agenda. For his part, Bishop could argue that the increased political involvement by people of all political stripes in the presidential campaign demonstrates how far the American people had retreated from political life.

Obama's assumption of the presidency comes at a time of intense national adversity. Such periods in the past, whether during the Great Depression, World War II or after the September 11 terrorist attacks, have coincided with periods of national unity.

The ensuing months and years will tell whether the sorting Bishop describes is overcome on the path to national unity and advancement or whether the excitement generated by the Obama campaign will be remembered as a temporary aberration in an increasingly divided nation.

IAN BURUMA'S MURDER IN AMSTERDAM

March 2, 2009

Murder always has the potential to shock, but this one was particularly gruesome.

On a cold Amsterdam morning in November 2004, Mohammed Bouyeri shot and killed Theo Van Gogh, great-grandnephew of the iconic painter. Witnesses talked later about the calm with which Bouyeri, a Muslim and the son of Moroccan immigrants, carried out his task. (He finished by taking a curved machete to his victim's throat, slitting it and then planting the machete in Van Gogh's chest.)

In addition to being a descendant of the great Dutch painter, Van Gogh was a prolific and controversial filmmaker who had collaborated with Somali émigré Ayaan Hirsi Ali on a film called *Submission*. In the note that he pinned to Van Gogh's chest, Bouyeri asserted that Hirsi Ali was a "soldier of Evil" who had "turned her back on the Truth." She, along with Holland, the United States, and an alleged Jewish cabal, would all be destroyed.

Van Gogh's murder rocked the nation that had long considered itself a bastion of tolerance.

The reverberations reached writer Ian Buruma, a Dutch national who left his home country at age 24 in 1975. Buruma's return to his native land and exploration of Holland during the time of the murder forms the basis for the provocative *Murder in Amsterdam: The Death of Theo Van Gogh and the Limits of Tolerance*.

The text is a rich one, filled with profiles of individuals: Hirsi Ali, whose story Buruma recounts in great detail; murdered right-wing politician Pim Fortuyn; and both protagonists in the drama. While the profiles are well-written and engaging, Buruma is not as concerned with individual stories as he is in showing how these people reflect, shape and collide with different strains of Dutch culture and identity.

Holland, according to Buruma, is at once a staid and volatile country. The arrival of large numbers of immigrants in several waves, a liberal tradition of welcoming foreigners, an ethos of acceptance of all kinds of behavior and shame at the nation's complicity with the Nazi regime during World War II are all significant ingredients in the stew of Dutch identity.

Buruma has spent much of his adult life in Asia and has a monthly commentary series called *Crossing Cultures*. His efforts to do just that in Holland are visible throughout the book, a work in which his linguistic dexterity and powers of observation are on full display. In a description of Hirsi Ali, for example, Buruma explains how her admirers and detractors view her before tracing her evolution from an observant and somewhat cowed Muslim woman to an outspoken and secular filmmaker.

He also has a fascinating section in which he describes the rise among Bouyeri's contemporaries, many of whom, like the murderer, are second-generation Muslims who identify as Dutch while hurling invective against the country and threatening its destruction.

Herein lies the rub that Holland confronts.

How does a country committed to openness and acceptance tolerate people who have no use for that value, and, in fact, denounce it as the symptom of a diseased society that must be destroyed?

Buruma does not answer the question, but the journey along the way to his ambiguous resolution makes for thought-provoking reading. Part of the value of *Murder in Amsterdam* is that one gets a primer on the intersections between Dutch immigration policy, conduct during World War II and the rise of Islamic fundamentalism as well as a meditation on how the ingredients in the spicy Dutch identity stew travel to other lands. Although the book is not about their country, readers in Denmark who lived through the cartoon controversy sparked by images of Mohammed may find themselves nodding while reading the work.

If there is to be a resolution, it may lie in the approach taken by Amsterdam Mayor Job Cohen. Buruma quotes a speech Cohen gave in which he linked the exclusion of his Jewish mother during World War II to that of Muslims today.

While commentators on several sides of the political divide and cultural spectrum criticized the mayor–Buruma notes that Cohen appeared in both Bouyeri's letters and as a target of Van Gogh's scathing attacks–his search for common ground may be the last best chance Holland and other nations have for finding accord with those who do not hew to their values and vision of society.

SEPT. 11 TERROR ATTACKS PROMPT JOHN PERKINS' CONFESSIONS

Nov. 27, 2009

The September 11 terror attacks "changed everything," according to some.

While the subsequent eight years have proven that initial assessment to be a bit overreaching, there is no denying the attacks' real impact on people throughout the world.

For the families of the victims, the death of their loved ones created a gaping and irreplaceable hole in the center of their lives.

For many in the United States, an illusion of security and invulnerability was permanently ruptured.

For other people, the attacks sparked actions that they had long considered, but not yet taken.

Childhood friend and award-winning photographer Andrew Lichtenstein married his then-longtime girlfriend Linda, for instance. The couple has since had two children.

And for John Perkins, a self-described "Economic Hit Man," the planes flying into the World Trade Center towers prompted him to complete *Confessions of an Economic Hit Man*, a work he had begun close to 20 years earlier, but deferred for several reasons.

The book's title is apt.

Perkins' work interweaves two related narrative strands.

The first is the role of hit men like him working for a few key companies to perpetuate the simultaneous economic and political domination of elites and environmental degradation and exploitation of the masses in the countries throughout the world.

In addition to MAIN, the company for which he worked, Perkins writes a lot about Bechtel and Halliburton.

The second is his personal journey, which began in a small and politically conservative New Hampshire town. Perkins writes about going through prep school at Tilton and an unsuccessful stint at Middlebury College before serving as a Peace Corps volunteer in Ecuador with his first wife. Through her uncle, Perkins gained admission to the far-flung world of the hit men that took him to Panama, Saudi Arabia, Iran and Iraq, among other countries.

Perkins is a skillful writer who knows how to turn a phrase and maintain a brisk pace. He has plenty of material to work with, too. At times, *Confessions* reads like a James Bond yarn, with the difference being Perkins is working to develop models of long-term economic growth that he and others use to convince government officials to accept. Padded with hefty profits for the contracting companies like Bechtel, the contracts also ensure the country's dim financial prospects and permanent indebtedness to financial institutions like the World Bank.

Confessions also provides brief historical background on the countries on which Perkins focuses before launching into his experiences in that country.

The chapter on Saudi Arabia takes places in 1974, shortly after the OPEC oil embargo that staggered the American economy. It sheds light not only on a massive money-laundering scheme, but on many of the relationships and forces in Saudi society that received so much attention in the aftermath of September 11.

At times, Perkins reminds the reader of an economically savvy Forrest Gump. He zips from country to country, forges relationships with novelist Graham Greene and General Omar Torrijos in Panama, reconnects with a college friend in Iran who tells him in the late 70s to leave the country, and returns in the early 2000s to Ecuador, where he had served in the Peace Corps 35 years earlier.

Perkins does not spare himself. He links the dulling of his ethical faculties to his immersion into the world of hit men. At different points in the book, he says that he helped to continue a system of slavery and was himself enslaved by the material goods and lifestyle to which he had access–the second claim is less convincing than the former.

Perkins credits a number of people, including a Colombian woman named Paula, for nudging him to consider the moral consequences of his actions. Looking at his inflated resume is one choice of many that moves Perkins to quit the agency in 1980.

The path to the book was far from a linear one.

Perkins started working on it after his second marriage and birth of his daughter Jessica, but decided instead to accept what amounted to a bribe to keep the project unfinished and unpublished.

He worked in the energy field for a time in the 80s, decided that advocating for nuclear energy was not the right thing to do and picked up the story after the two planes flew into the towers.

Confessions contains an epilogue, recommendations for action, and a timeline of key personal and professional events in Perkins' life. He closes the work by citing Tom Paine in *Common Sense* and Thomas Jefferson's fabled words to begin the *Declaration of Independence*.

In the end, *Confessions* pulls back the veil on the workings of the global economic system from the late 60s to the 80s, with a reminder in the epilogue that Bechtel and Halliburton's strong connections to the Reagan and Bush White Houses remain deep. This is the book's most distinctive and sobering aspect. The confessional dimension works less well, but brings the reader along to the end.

Perkins' words may not be enough to undo his actions. Still, we should be glad that the terror attacks moved him to finish the project he had begun after his daughter's birth.

WAGE THEFT WARRIOR KIM BOBO'S NEW BOOK

Jan. 9, 2009

Millions of people across America are having part or all of their pay stolen by their employers, but Kim Bobo is doing something about it.

The founding director of Interfaith Worker Justice since 1996, Bobo is working with worker centers around the country to wage a campaign against the widespread crime that takes many different forms.

She's also written a book.

In *Wage Theft in America: Why Millions of Working Americans Are Not Getting Paid-And What We Can Do About It*, Bobo explains wage theft's origins, forms and extent before articulating a new vision of the Department of Labor and identifying concrete actions individuals and organizations can take against this nationwide epidemic.

Full disclosure: IWJ Communications Coordinator Danny Postel is a close friend.

Bobo begins the book by describing the forms wage theft takes. These range from having employees work through lunch and other breaks to not paying overtime to making workers pay payroll taxes to simply refusing to pay workers.

She then explains some of the reasons why employers take these actions–greed, racism and sexism figure prominently here–and how current U.S. law fails to protect workers. These failures include a paltry enforcement staff, laws that differ across states and legislation that lacks sufficient punch, she says.

The result is that millions of people across the country, many of whom are already at the bottom of the economic ladder, do not receive their just wages and have less recourse than they should if they choose to pursue what has been stolen from them.

The second part of the book focuses on what individuals and organizations, particularly unions and worker centers, can do to stop the abuse.

216 Meaningful Matters: Reflections on Joy, Loss and Our Changing World

Bobo provides plenty of concrete suggestions for people to get involved, from direct interaction with workers' organizations to advocacy with elected officials.

Bobo includes a chapter on the life and work of the late Frances Perkins, whose service in the 30s and 40s as Secretary of Labor under President Franklin Delano Roosevelt made her the first female cabinet member in American history, as well as a chapter on an alternative vision of the Department of Labor. Bobo advocates for more wage cops, wage and hour partnerships and a multi-faceted approach to workers' education–measures that, if adopted, would make the agency more responsive to workers' needs.

She closes the book on an optimistic note:

"The national epidemic of wage theft is not inevitable. A hundred and fifty years ago, we didn't know if we could end slavery. We did. A hundred years ago, few thought we could stop child labor in industries. We did ... Ending wage theft will not be easy, but together we can put a stop to it and rebuild protections and standards for workers. Ending wage theft is good for workers, good for ethical business, and good for America."

A series of helpful appendices, which mirror the book's trajectory, follows this statement. Bobo provides attentive readers with a list of wage theft settlements and private suits, four appendices filled with resources and a study guide for the book.

Wage Theft in America has many strengths.

More than many books about workers, this book is designed to help spur people to action while providing them with the ideas and resources they need. As part of this intention, the tone is conversational and informative. Bobo also makes sure to present her information in digestible, self-contained bites and to offer plenty of practical suggestions.

The book's structure merits praise on several levels.

Bobo strikes an effective balance between providing a clear-eyed look at the problem and its consequences while also showing the possibility of constructive action. This is an impressive feat: too much of the former can demoralize the reader, while excessive doses of the latter can make the author seem Pollyannaish and disconnected from many people's daily realities. The anecdotes of current workers and historic figures like Perkins contribute to this positive aspect of Bobo's work.

Bobo demonstrates a fair-minded approach toward employers by stating more than once that many do act in honorable ways and even calling for those who act with honor to be saluted for doing so. These statements give her critique and suggestions credibility because they illustrate an emphasis on reaching constructive real-world outcomes rather than posturing in the name of ideological purity.

Finally, no discussion of the book's strengths would be complete without mentioning Bobo's efforts to place a campaign against wage theft in the context of faith traditions. This is a theme she carries throughout the book from the introduction to the epigraphs for each chapter to one of the appendices, where she includes many denominations' positions of wages and working conditions.

This linkage of ancient Jewish, Christian and Muslim quotations to current contexts shows the timeless nature of the challenge Bobo says must be met and shifts the campaign from being one about wage retrieval and prevention to a continuation of a faith-based struggle for justice.

Such positioning elevates the campaign's moral ground–this is not to suggest that the quest absent the faith tradition is less noble–and can have the effect of drawing in people who might otherwise shy away from joining such an effort for fear of seeming too radical.

The book is not without challenges.

The description of the societal challenges impacting workers and employers is quite thin. Bobo covers globalization and America's unresolved immigration situation in a combined three paragraphs, for instance. While such brevity is understandable given that section's broader purpose of articulating employers' and workers' societal context, it is so short as to provide neither insight nor anything but the most general of understandings.

In a similar vein, Bobo moves from Moses' proposed three-day strike against Pharaoh to eighteenth century American craft guilds to nineteenth century textile mills in consecutive paragraphs.

In addition, while Bobo does provide plenty of evidence in much of the book, at times she presents broad assertions without any supporting documentation.

At one point, for example, she writes, "When unions represent most workers in an industry, wage theft is virtually eliminated" before going on to suggest that all workers in garment, poultry and nursing home industries be represented by unions.

As a former teacher's union representative, member of the union's negotiating team and general labor supporter, I agree with Bobo's recommendation. However, I found myself wishing that she provided examples for her assertion about the elimination of wage theft. Such evidence would have buttressed her point, while an explanation of how the theft was stopped could have been worthy of an entire chapter in itself.

These difficulties notwithstanding, *Wage Theft in America* is a valuable contribution to exposing and helping to solve a little-discussed problem that afflicts millions of American workers, their families and their communities. *Wage Theft* will not stop the practice by itself. But it will undoubtedly inform and inspire those people who seek to make Bobo's optimistic vision a reality.

DAVE CULLEN ON
THE COLUMBINE SHOOTINGS

June 8, 2009

Dave Cullen spent a decade writing Columbine.
(Photograph by Genevieve Lee of TrueLee Photography)

Ten years later, images from the Columbine shootings remain seared into our collective memory.

The bloodied library floor.

The crying high school students holding each other in utter shock.

President Clinton yet again denouncing the senseless violence of another school shooting – this one, the most violent and bloody in American history.

Reporter Dave Cullen was there from the beginning and has followed the story with remarkable stamina, persistence, insight and commitment during the ensuing decade. His book, *Columbine*, published around the shootings' tenth anniversary, provides the most comprehensive and authoritative look available at killers Eric Harris and Dylan Klebold, at the buildup to the shootings and their ruinous aftermath, and at the elusive question of why.

To be transparent, Cullen and I are both Dart Center Ochberg Fellows. Named for Dr. Frank Ochberg, a psychiatrist who is a strong presence in the book whose research led to the coining of the phrase "Stockholm syndrome." The fellowships provide a space to help journalists who cover trauma and violence deal with those issues in their stories and with themselves. Cullen and I are also serving as judges in a journalism competition.

Irony pulses through *Columbine* from the opening pages, which start not with the shootings, but the weekend before. Principal Frank DeAngelis urges the students to come back safely after the prom the following weekend.

Cullen swings the storytelling pendulum back and forth throughout the work, which has two major narrative strands. The first tells about the boys' childhoods, histories, personalities and eventual decision to carry out their gruesome plan. The second details the shootings' multifold and devastating consequences.

Cullen had a difficult task as a writer.

On the one hand, he was writing about an event that was covered, as he notes, less than half an hour after the shootings started. Columbine has been the subject of endless analysis, speculation, books, movies and even legislation. This made it extremely difficult to bring new information into the conversation.

At the same time, Cullen also confronted a number of myths that sprang up about the shootings. These ranged from the idea that the killers were seeking revenge against jocks who bullied them to the assertion that one of the victims, Cassie Bernall, told one of the boys she believed in God in the instant before she was killed.

Cullen pulls off both masterfully. In part, this is because he sifted through tens of thousands of documents, among them files from law enforcement and the killers' diaries. He also immersed himself in several branches of psychology and conducted hundreds, if not thousands, of interviews with people affected by the shootings.

One of his major findings was that far from being bullied and cowed victims members of the Trenchcoat Mafia who killed in a spontaneous moment, Eric Harris was a psychopath while Dylan Klebold was his depressive, suicidal follower. The pair wrote and talked about their plans, which were hatched more than a year in advance of the actual event. Their goals were far larger than the biggest school shooting in history; they wanted to blow up the entire building, and tried repeatedly to do so while shooting their fellow students.

Beyond insight into the killers' psychological makeup, Cullen does a meticulous job of showing the failings of adults along the way to recognize and take corrective action to thwart Harris and Klebold's deadly plan. He also reveals an attempted cover-up by the Jefferson County Sheriff's Office.

In some ways, these are the most painful sections of the book to read.

The mother of a boy who was threatened by Harris contacted law enforcement multiple times to share her concerns. An English teacher, after reading a disturbing essay by Klebold, spoke with the boy, called his parents and notified his guidance counselor.

Nothing was done.

Cullen blends dispassion and compassion in his description of Tom and Sue Klebold, Dylan's parents, who have been far more forthcoming than the Harrises, who have never agreed to be interviewed. Cullen brings these same qualities to characters like Patrick Ireland, who was shot but not killed, during the rampage. He also writes with insight about DeAngelis, who lost his marriage and much of the faculty's backing, and the pastor whose spiritual support of the Klebolds contributed to his leaving his position a year later.

Cullen's attention to detail is another praiseworthy aspect of the book.

Chilling and poignant details abound on *Columbine's* pages.

These include the recounting of the final words Sue Klebold exchanged with her son–he had enjoyed the steak he had at Outback Steakhouse, Harris' favorite restaurant–to the last of the Basement Tapes the boys recorded before heading off on their fateful mission. The book contains a minute-by-minute re-creation of the shootings, including their suicides, a description of the achingly slow rehabilitation process Ireland goes through and Sue Klebold's conclusion that Dylan's actions were contrary to how she and her husband had raised him.

These details are testament to Cullen's intimate knowledge of his material and his considerable skill as a writer.

Columbine is not without minor imperfections.

While effective, the alternating narrative threads can be a bit jarring at the beginning as one is getting oriented to the work. Cullen's background as a daily reporter shows through in patches of jaunty prose that do not work quite as well as others.

And the reader, at the end of the book, is left still not understanding why the boys took their murderous actions.

The last point is not a criticism of Cullen's work, but rather a reminder that understanding pure evil–whether in the form of the Holocaust, the Khmer Rouge, or South Africa's apartheid regime–remains elusive. That Cullen, after a decade of hard-spent work, is not able to arrive at a compelling and convincing answer is not an indictment of his work, but a reminder of how difficult that quest can be.

Cullen ends the book with the unveiling of a memorial close to eight years after the shootings and the release of hundreds of doves into the air. The coming to order in the air of these birds associated with peace is a reminder that, after all, life does go on. As Patrick Ireland says at one point in the book, a moment of tragedy does not define an individual, a community, or a nation's entire life.

That Harris and Klebold were able to carry out their horrific plans should continue to challenge us to seek to understand, to meet our children's needs and to prevent further similar atrocities.

The fruit of 10 years of Cullen's life, *Columbine* is an authoritative account and resource to help us do that necessary work.

PHILIP ZIMBARDO EXPLORES HOW GOOD PEOPLE CAN TURN EVIL

July 12, 2009

Instances of evil are all too easy to find these days.

Whether it's in the degrading images of blindfolded nude Iraqi prisoners stacked on top of each other while a grinning Lynndie England smiles at the camera at the notorious Abu Ghraib prison, the murder of hundreds of thousands of Tutsis in Rwanda in 1994, or the ongoing killing in Darfur, examples of man's inhumanity to man abound.

The question of why these abuses continue to occur in different parts of the world is far more difficult to answer than pointing out their existence.

It's not for a lack of trying.

Some people cite the essential depravity of human nature, while others invoke the "few bad apples theory." In her famous and controversial work, *Eichmann in Jerusalem*, Hannah Arendt coined the often-invoked phrase, "the banality of evil."

Philip Zimbardo has a different take.

The emeritus Stanford University Psychology professor had his own memorable experiences with overseeing an experiment that turned evil in his 1971 Stanford Prison Experiment.

The experiment involved paid volunteers who were divided into prisoners and guards. It was slated to last two weeks, but Zimbardo shut it down after six days at his then-girlfriend and later-wife's urging.

Among the many elements that stunned Zimbardo was how the speed with which his subjects, college-age men, absorbed their respective identities. A prisoner rebellion occurred on the second day. A prisoner introduced into the group after the experiment began a hunger strike.

On the guards' side, each of the men acting in that capacity either committed or silently witnessed abusive treatment of the prisoners.

I took an introductory psychology class from Zimbardo in 1984 and remember vividly his description of the experiment, which took place in the very building in which he was lecturing to me and the close to 300 other students in the class.

After class ended, I went outside into the hallway where he had just described the terrible events that had happened and tried to imagine what that had been like for the participants. It was not quite like visiting a ghost town, but rather like trying to picture where the ghosts had walked and talked and breathed while alive.

Zimbardo uses the prison experiment and the lessons he learned from it as the basis to explore broader questions of human behavior in *The Lucifer Effect: Understanding How Good People Turn Evil.*

Zimbardo's essential contention is that people are influenced by the situations and systems in which they find themselves. In many cases, the power of the situation is strong enough for people to override standards for appropriate behavior in some experiments or to ignore their judgments of right behavior and perpetrate cruelty to others.

From my experience with him, Zimbardo is a fan of art and music. On the last psychology class he taught us, he played Don McClean's song "Vincent" while showing us images of Vincent Van Gogh's work.

He frames *the Lucifer Effect* with M.C. Escher's image, "Circle Limit IV," in which white angels and black horned demons of differing sizes mingle in a circle. Zimbardo does this to show that people's nature contains the capacity for both good and evil and that the situation makes a powerful difference in influencing people's choices.

Most of the first half of the book is devoted to a more than 200-page recap of the prison experiment, starting with the "arrest'" of the prisoners–Zimbardo claims that even with the arrest, these participants gave informed consent–and moving through the rebellion, the weathering of parental visits, the descent into constant prisoner abuse, and his heeding the words of Christina Maslach, who insisted that terrible things were happening to those boys.

At the end of that part of the book, Zimbardo asks the question whether the experiment had been unethical and finds himself culpable on absolute moral grounds. He writes that he bears responsibility as the experiment's architect. He has apologized to the people he harmed in the experiment and continues to do so.

Yet he also argues that the experiment can be considered ethical on a more relative ethical scale and goes on to list all the benefits he believes have accrued from what he calls the "SPE." These benefits range from helping the individuals who participated in it as prisoners and researchers to its being cited in cultural and professional arenas, according to Zimbardo.

From there, he moves to a broader consideration of the factors that contribute to the situations that seem to exert such power over people. People familiar with Stanley Milgram's experiments on obedience, the Kitty Genovese case and high school history teacher Ron Jones' *Third Wave* will likely move quickly through this section. He adds to the tendency of obedience the power of anonymity and of dehumanization in increasing situational power and loosening social restraints.

Zimbardo then launches into an extensive exploration of the prisoner abuses at Abu Ghraib, where he contends many of the psychological dynamics that operated in the SPE also came into play. Furthermore, this section presents his most thorough explanation of the military as an example of a system, pointing out how the consequences meted out by the military focused on the direct perpetrators and not on their supervisors.

He includes in this section a discussion of torture of terror suspects and a restatement of people that Human Rights Watch said should be tried for those actions, adding Vice President Dick Cheney and President George W. Bush to the list the group compiled.

The book's final section looks at different forms of heroism.

Zimbardo notes that whether cultivating obedience toward heroic behavior can be encouraged has not been studied and articulates a framework to identify a dozen types of heroes who operate in military, civil and social areas. These heroes are linked by taking significant risks for the good of others and without expectation of reward, he says. Some take their actions in a single moment, while others act this way for a lifetime.

Zimbardo writes that he includes this part of the book at the end to provide an uplifting conclusion to what he says is a difficult and draining journey.

I remember Zimbardo as having a hefty ego, and it does not appear to have diminished over the years. He includes multiple glowing letters about the prison experiment and often notes the praise that others have heaped on his landmark work.

This somewhat off-putting tendency notwithstanding, he does deserve credit for pointing out similar underlying psychological dynamics in a number of historical situations and for arguing strongly, if not completely persuasively, about the importance of the situation on people's actions.

That said, *The Lucifer Effect* does have a number of problems.

These begin with factual inaccuracies that undermine his credibility to write authoritatively about different historical moments. He writes that Nelson Mandela was imprisoned for 27 years on Robben Island after being put on trial in 1962. In fact, Mandela was sentenced in 1964. While incarcerated for 27 years, he served his time in several different prisons.

Zimbardo also makes assertions about Milgram's experiment that strain credulity. He writes that changing the initial experiment's location from Yale University to a less prestigious site reduced obedience rates from 65 to 47 percent–a result he says was not statistically significant. Later in the section he asserts that Milgram's results did not vary meaningfully by country, even though the obedience rate of Australian participants was 28 percent while that of South Africans was 88 percent!

These statements appear hard to believe, if not outright ridiculous.

A more troubling element is how Zimbardo appears comfortable applying full moral scrutiny to those who were responsible for the misdeeds at Abu Ghraib while putting his own ethical failures into an introductory section on ethics that later is trumped by the positive results to which he says his experiment contributed. He even writes that a high-ranking military official's assumption of responsibility for what happened at Abu Ghraib is meaningless without some formal consequence, yet does not seem to think that anything similar should have happened to him.

Zimbardo would likely point out that there are major differences between an academic experiment and sanctioned abuse and torture of American prisoners of war. His accuracy in making that point underscores the most basic problem with his explanation: it is so general as to be applicable in every situation, and, therefore, of limited utility.

Zimbardo's assertion that the basic psychological patterns are the same whether for Jim Jones in Guyana, the Stanford Prison Experiment, Abu Ghraib, Rwanda and Milgram's experiments, apartheid South Africa or Nazi-era Germany ignores the specific aspects of each moment that contributed to their different outcomes and does not allow us to make meaningful distinctions between them.

The irony, of course, is that Zimbardo cites the distinction between experiment and "reality" to evade facing real consequences for the abuse he oversaw while running the prison experiment.

In short, if the concept of the Person, the Situation and the System is a brush, it is too broad and paints only one color.

These problems do not mean that one should not read the book, but rather than one should do so with a critical eye. Being reminded of our capacity for evil through action or bystanding is something that we would all do well to heed, even if we are using a flawed tool for that purpose.

SUDHIR VENKATESH'S VIVID DESCRIPTION, INCOMPLETE RECKONING

Jan. 8, 2009

Sudhir Venkatesh depicts life on Chicago's streets in Gang Leader for a Day.
(Photo courtesy of the Charles H. Revson Foundation)

Sudhir Venkatesh's first trip to the Robert Taylor Homes, once the nation's largest housing project, is the stuff of legend.

A newly-minted graduate student in sociology at the University of Chicago, the Indian-born Californian walked up to residents at the notorious housing project holding a survey from MacArthur Award-winning professor William Julius Wilson.

"What does it feel like to be black and poor?" read the first question which Venkatesh asked the residents to answer.

Far from responding, Venkatesh's subjects held him hostage for close to a day, debating whether to kill him before releasing him with a clear warning not to return.

Steven Levitt told the story first in the bestselling *Freakonomics*, which included a chapter about the economics of drug dealing based on data Venkatesh said he got during his subsequent research.

Gang Leader for A Day: A Rogue Sociologist Takes to the Streets is Venkatesh's turn to tell his own story of that first day as well as of many of the others that followed during his six years of doctoral research. And tell it he does in a book that intrigues with its memorable and intricate description of a community many people never enter, yet disappoints with its incomplete moral reckoning.

Venkatesh's relationship with J.T., a Black Kings leader, is at the book's center.

It is J.T. who intervenes on Venkatesh's behalf to end his hostage saga. After finding the pluck to go back to Robert Taylor, Venkatesh gains access, with J.T.'s approval, to the projects and much of the gang's operations. Venkatesh makes it clear that the gangs see themselves as community leaders, providing jobs, mediating disputes and keeping order in the area in a way that no one else can. Venkatesh discusses the violence he hears about, witnesses, and, in one instance, even participates in, while also discussing the managerial structure and continual decisions a leader must make.

The relationship with J.T. is not an easy one for many reasons, and J.T. makes it clear early in the story that Venkatesh must decide whether he is with J.T. or with other elements of the community. (Venkatesh branches out, but appears comforted when J.T. later writes a letter of introduction to East Coast gang members that says, in essence, "Sudhir is with me.") Venkatesh depicts in extensive detail the myriad mundane decisions gang leaders must make and the violence that underpins relationships within the gang and in the community.

J.T. comes to trust Venkatesh, believing that Venkatesh is writing a book about his life, and supplies him with access to events that would otherwise be impossible to attend. The title, which is a bit misleading, refers to a day when the gang chief and his associates appoint Venkatesh the leader for a day–but only after they have accepted his unwillingness to mete out or assign physical punishment. Within the parameters he has established for himself, Venkatesh's judgment and instincts are solid, according to J.T.

Although central to the narrative, J.T. is just one of many characters in *Gang Leader for a Day*. Other memorable people include T-Bone, the gang's bookish accountant who supplies Venkatesh with four years of records of the gang's finances; J.T.'s warm-hearted mother, always ready with a smile, a plate of home-cooked food and homespun wisdom; and Ms. Bailey, the Local Advisory Council leader and one of the most complex people in the book.

Ms. Bailey tends to the needs of the families in her building by dealing with the gangs. In one memorable scene, she chews out Venkatesh when he feels she has been hoodwinked by a drugged mother whose children Venkatesh buys groceries for, telling him that no one in her building goes hungry. Because he had such extensive access, Venkatesh is able to create the feeling of an entire world in which strong community ties and chilling violence coexist, in which cops are more feared than criminals and in which connection to political leadership and traditional resources is nonexistent.

Based on research Venkatesh did from 1989 to 1996, *Gang Leader for A Day* is by far Venkatesh's most personal work to date. *American Project: The Rise and Fall of a Modern Ghetto* was converted from his dissertation and told the history of the Robert Taylor Homes from its inception through its planned destruction under the Chicago Housing Authority's Plan For Transformation. While a major contribution to several bodies of literature and far more readable than many converted dissertations, the book was far from intimate in tone and substance.

Off The Books: The Underground Economy of the Urban Poor, an examination of the underground economy in "Marquis Park," the thinly veiled pseudonym of a South Side neighborhood, was Venkatesh's second look at the community, and one in which his voice appeared more often. To his credit, Venkatesh includes a number of excerpts of interviews in which residents tell him that, despite his having been in the community for years, he still "doesn't know shit."

Gang Leader For A Day's signature strength is in its depiction of the world inside the Robert Taylor Homes and of the gang members' lives. Far from being caricatures, many people in Venkatesh's book have hidden desires for a different path that often do not get realized. One gang member confesses that he wants to leave the gang and start teaching dance, for instance.

Venkatesh also shows just how tricky moral judgments can be, especially when applied by an outsider to the community. As in *Off the Books*, Venkatesh includes the voices of women who prostitute themselves to help pay for their children's needs and are not judged by the community, while a drug-consuming mother who does not tend to her children is.

Venkatesh does not back away from depicting his own moral quandaries, which are many and, at times, unanticipated. An example of the latter comes when he shares the substance of his conversations with residents about their underground economic activities with J.T. and Ms. Bailey. This leads to the pair shaking down residents for money they didn't know was coming in and to Venkatesh being perceived as a snitch. Venkatesh's years-long misleading of J.T. about his plans to write about him is another. (He appears to have written the book in part to honor his earlier commitment.)

But the most basic dilemma, of course, is how Venkatesh strikes an uneasy balance between his fascination with gang life, his admiration for J.T.'s charisma and leadership and his revulsion at the violence that undergirds their community control and the drug dealing that drives their income. At different times in the book, Venkatesh takes solace in also being seen as a hustler of a different stripe who won't take no for an answer. Another source of comfort is J.T.'s having left the gang and gone straight while appearing not to be bitter that Venkatesh has continued on his path toward academic stardom and moved on to other research subjects.

Venkatesh does an effective job of articulating the moral challenges he encounters, but he does far less well reckoning with the implications of what he has seen and learned for his responsibilities as a scholar, a citizen and his allegiance to his moral code. This is a significant omission, both because his insights would be valuable and because judgment of these actions raises questions of responsibility and accountability for Venkatesh and the people with whom he interacts.

Ironically, several of the residents nudge Venkatesh in that direction. One woman states emphatically the first time she meets him: Don't treat us as victims. We know what we are doing.

Venkatesh, however, does not apply the same standards to himself. While he would be overstepping his boundaries were he to offer sweeping conclusions that could be applied from his experience, his failure to point the same compass at himself that the woman urges him to apply to community residents leaves an unsatisfying taste in the reader's mouth.

A vivid description of a world many people never see, and one that has been altered fundamentally with the destruction of the Robert Taylor Homes through the housing authority's plan, *Gang Leader for A Day* feels in the end more an exercise in personal catharsis than moral reflection and confrontation.

AFROREGGAE A SIGN OF HOPE IN RIO'S FAVELAS

Feb. 7, 2010

At the end of the one of the chapters in Patrick Neate and Damian Platt's *Culture Is Our Weapon*, the authors insert "a simple statistic."

From 1948 to 1999, about 13,000 people died in the Israeli-Palestinian conflict, they say.

By contrast, close to four times that number died due to violence in Brazil's favelas from 1979 to 2000.

This data gives a smidgen of insight into the favelas' perilous world–an existence the authors flesh out by describing the inexorable pull of "o trafficante," or drug traffic, the murderous behavior of the police, and the official neglect by Brazil's social and political elite of the favelas since their inception close to a century ago.

More than 2 million people, the majority of whom are black, live in the favelas, a collection of illegal residences often tolerated by the government.

At the same time, as in America, some of the most dire living circumstances can be the environment of the most dynamic art, cultural expression and movements for social change.

In their book, Neate and Platt trace the history and current actions of AfroReggae, a combination non-profit, nurturer and promoter of artistic talent and mediator of violent disputes in the favelas.

The music style arose after the 1993 Vigario Geral massacre of more than two dozen civilians by police. A fusion of African and reggae music, with local flavor thrown in for good measure, AfroReggae has been a way for people to depict and describe the experience of life in the favelas.

The non-profit emerged from this period after an initial period as a newspaper. While the group alters its approach depending on the conditions and needs of the favela's residents, the goals of promoting peace, jobs and general social uplift have remained consistent.

Neate and Platt state that they are not journalists but rather are admirers of the organization's work. The result is a favorable, if not uncritical, look at the organization and what it does. The book is a bit short on details about AfroReggae's efficacy, but it is clear from the book that there are many people who join the group who would otherwise be involved in drug dealing and on their way to an early death.

"How It Works" is one of the book's bleakest chapters.

It describes the almost inevitable pull trafficking, violence and mayhem can exert on the favela's youth. The chapter tells the story of Jorge, a promising son of a single mother who must work multiple jobs to make ends meet. This leaves Jorge in the care of his grandmother, who soon starts to lose the boy to the streets. Through the course of the chapter the boy is drawn deeper and deeper into the drug trade, killing first a boy from a rival faction and then one he knows, all by age 15.

Another dark chapter talks about the rampant corruption among the police, many of whom make so little money they must accept bribes to survive and whose children hide their parents' law enforcement work for fear of being targeted for reprisals.

The book is not all gloom and doom.

AfroReggae includes chapters about survivors and about the group's at times effective interventions into the rampant violence.

In the end, life in the favelas, and AfroReggae's efforts to change it, continue unabated. The group has victories big and as agonizingly small as having just a few moments or hours of peace. Their triumphs underscore the scale of the obstacles the community confronts, the courage the group brings to meet them and the value of Neale and Platt's book in bringing their story to the larger world.

LINDA NATHAN TACKLES SCHOOL'S HARDEST QUESTIONS

Jan. 25, 2010

Linda Nathan, center, talks with students from Boston Arts Academy,
the school she founded.
(Photograph by Tom Kates)

Linda Nathan is an education warrior.

The unassuming educator and wife of friend and Tufts University Lecturer Steve Cohen has dedicated her adult life to Boston's youth, pushing them to realize their often untapped potential against considerable adversity.

Since 1998, the former director of Fenway Middle College has been the founder and head of Boston Arts Academy, a public high school in which

236   Meaningful Matters: Reflections on Joy, Loss and Our Changing World

students learn a traditional curriculum and have an artistic focus or major that they pursue.

Since its inception, Boston Arts Academy has placed about 95 percent of its graduates in college-a level far higher than the system-wide figure of 50 percent.

As impressive as that statistic is, it may not be the most compelling aspect of the school, according to Nathan.

It's the questioning.

Nathan and the dedicated staff she has assembled are committed to a relentless interrogation of things small and large at the school and to transmitting that culture of inquiry to their students.

Nathan distills and shares the wisdom she has accrued during the past quarter century in *The Hardest Questions Aren't on the Test*, a passionate testimony to the community that she has played a pivotal role in creating at Boston Arts.

Nathan divides the book into three sections and six chapters, each of which has a framing question. The sections are dedicated to school structure, supporting teachers and addressing inequality–roles that she asserts are critical for school leaders to do. (She has an entertaining and thoughtful critique of how principals are portrayed in many Hollywood movies about teachers.)

The Hardest Questions has many positive features.

Nathan devotes a chapter early in the book to describing interactions between two ace teachers and their students. She makes it clear that the teachers are demanding and accepting, strong and flexible.

Nathan also stresses that these two instructors are exceptional examples, but that she could have cited many others in the building. Beyond that, these teachers gain strength because they are not stars seeking their own individual praise and honors, rather they are part of a team. (A gifted music teacher who is not committed to the team concept is asked to leave.)

The team is characterized by its honesty.

Nathan offers numerous examples of hers and others' efforts to surmount the visible and invisible barriers her students confront on the way to academic success and artistic fulfillment.

One of the book's most poignant moments comes when she describes a talented female student's losing out on a full scholarship to a prestigious conservatory because she was too ashamed of her inability to pay the $500 deposit to share her need with anyone on staff.

Nathan also talks about her awkward attempt to diversify the composition of the parent advisory group. She describes how, after the nominations had been submitted, she noticed that only one parent of color was among the ranks of 15 or so people in the group. Her suggestion that the committee reopen the process led to understandably hard feelings, several parents walking out and the threat of a lawsuit.

She persisted, and the group's composition did indeed become more diverse.

You sense that Nathan feels comfortable with that stance; and, to her credit, she also talks about moments when she made choices of which she is far less proud.

In a chapter about how the school in 2002 confronted hateful graffiti, for example, she writes about how she was far less morally outraged and active in confronting a similar homophobic incident. Her willingness to share her less impressive choices enhances Nathan's credibility and moral integrity.

Nathan also describes the at times interminable staff discussions about how best to deal with students' home lives, cultures and communities in which they live. She writes about the frustration many staff members felt at the number and length of the conversations, which for months did not lead to any concrete action.

She explains that there are limits to the discourse, too.

White students who feel that they are being blamed for historic and current racism do not appear to receive much sympathy at Boston Arts. Nathan writes that she is shocked when a student approaches her after the Gulf War began in 2003 to ask for information about why one might support President Bush's decision–a request that surprised Nathan because she considered it self-evident that the war was a wrong one. Even though she later convened a teach-in, it's clear that the ground in Boston Arts is not neutral.

Nathan also devotes a certain amount of space throughout the book and in the conclusion to explaining the central elements–a set of shared values; a collection of talented and dedicated teachers; and a series of culminating projects–that lead to the school's success and that offer whatever lessons she feels the school has to offer.

The writing is straightforward, laced with anecdotes and peppered with personal reflections.

But you don't read *The Hardest Questions* for the writing.

Rather the strongest impression that emerges from the work is one of an experienced, innovative and intelligent school leader sharing her bone-deep pride in her staff and the students they have helped usher through adolescence and toward their dreams.

HONOR FOR ALL RALLY IN WASHINGTON, D.C.

June 25, 2011

They came from across the country.

Some drove.

Others flew.

Still others rode motorcycles.

But whatever their mode of transportation, all of the people who attended the Honor for All rally today on the Senate side of the U.S. Capitol building shared a common purpose: to make visible the invisible wounds sustained by veterans and their families, and to honor all of them for their contributions to the nation.

Organized by Tom Mahany, a clear-eyed, blond-haired stone mason and Vietnam veteran from Michigan, the event began right at 10:00 a.m. and continued in a punctual manner throughout the day.

The weather cooperated. A few clouds dotted the blue sky while the temperature peaked in the low 80s.

The crowd was small and many of the chairs were unfilled, but Dart Society founder and psychiatrist Frank Ochberg was undaunted. "Empty chairs don't hurt us; they tell us how far we have to go," he said.

Mahany opened the presentations by paying tribute to his brother-in-law who killed himself 20 years ago after waging a 15-year struggle with depression and Post-Traumatic Stress Disorder (PTSD).

His point, and that of other speakers like Gregg Keesling, whose son also took his life: soldiers who kill themselves after combat should be accorded the same honor and acknowledgment as those who died on the battlefield.

Keesling, who sports a reddish pony tail, said he urged his son to get help for the psychological torment he was enduring, but heard the all-too-common refrain that to ask for help is a sign of weakness, not strength.

The father took aim at the current practice of the military not sending condolence letters to military families whose loved ones commit suicide.

Honor For All aims to reverse that and marshaled an impressive array of speakers to present their case.

Brigadier Generals Michael Miller and Richard Thomas spoke about the military's commitment to helping soldiers dealing with these issues.

Ochberg spoke about a Vietnam veteran named Terry whose wife Cathy approached him to help her husband. For 40 years Terry had blamed himself for his friend's death.

Yet through his conversations with the psychiatrist he found another way to think about his experience.

Rather than causing his death, Terry, who is religious, started to think about himself as delivering his friend to his Lord.

Terry and Cathy held each other and wept as Ochberg spoke about them and their story.

Several other speakers addressed the role and impact on the family.

Lucretia Bellamy, whose husband is convalescing at Walter Reed, declared her love for all veterans and her insistence that no one disrespect them.

"My name is Lucretia Bellamy and I roar with the roar of a lioness," she exclaimed.

Military wife Kristina Kaufman spoke about the number of spouses who committed suicide because of the stress caused by being married to their husbands after their return.

She named three women who were her friends. She did so, she said, to give them their dignity.

Politicians like U.S. Sen. Daniel Inouye, a member of the 442 Regimental Combat Team who lost his arm during World War II, sent a message he had delivered to a staff this member at 7:30 a.m. this morning.

Other politicians like U.S. Sen. Kent Conrad and U.S. Rep. Andre Carson also emphasized the importance of the cause.

Keynote speakers Jeremiah Workman and Jennifer Crane shared their stories of trying to drown their pain in alcohol and drugs, of losing almost everything and of finding their way out from the abyss.

For both, a turning point came when they accepted that they had PTSD and a traumatic brain injury and got help.

Representatives from the non-profit sector addressed the crowd as did trauma survivors and former soldiers turned writers like Dario DiBattista.

In the end, Mahany returned and called up his nephew Brian, the son of his brother-in-law.

Now 30, the younger man and his uncle shared a long embrace.

The open expression of emotion and the movement from the invisible wounds that contributed to Brian's father's death into the comforting of his son symbolized the hope and promise of the day and the movement.

I have not served in the military and will never do so. I am by temperament and practice someone who believes in non-violence.

Yet the courage of today's speakers–the catch in their throats, the limp in their walks and the exquisite tenderness with which two Marine parents, whose son is struggling with these issues, asked Jennifer Crane if they could hug her–brought home to me as never before the valor of the men and women who have, as one speaker said, written a blank check to the country.

They deserve our respect, and they deserve our honor.

I SHOULD HAVE LISTENED TO DUNREITH

Dec. 3, 2011

Journalist Lorenzo Morales and I were roommates at the climate change conference in Durban, South Africa in 2011.
(Photo courtesy of Lorenzo Morales)

As with many things in my life, I should have listened to my wife.

This particular lesson came as I was packing to attend the United Nations Framework on Climate Change Conference.

"You look like you're planning to move there," she said.

I had to admit that she had a point.

My college days of traveling through Europe with just a backpack and sleeping bag seemed as if they never had existed. The metal seams on my black carry-on suitcase looked strained beyond their capacity and about to burst at any second. I had yet to put in my blazer, shoes, black and white socks or pajamas.

This said nothing of the work and personal laptops, 20 batteries for my flip camera, or three hard cover books about climate change that I was planning to stuff into my backpack, which, if it could talk, would express the identical distress as my suitcase's seams.

Rather than heed her sage input, I upped the ante.

"I'll want to have room to bring back some of the materials I get there," I said after I returned from the basement with a full-sized suitcase to hold my wares. "Besides, the copies of Hoy I'm planning to give everyone are taking up a lot of room."

"Uh-huh," my wife said, her arched eyebrows conveying her skepticism. "It's your trip, so do what you want."

I realized her wisdom after I arrived, got to my room at the Gateway Hotel and met Lorenzo Morales, my roommate from Colombia, an accomplished journalist and a very polite person.

I could not be sure as we had just met, and he appeared to register some surprise at the unending stream of items that issued forth from my suitcase.

Where I brought two laptops, he brought one.

Where I brought enough clothes to avoid doing laundry, he brought a supply that would serve him just fine and require him to do some minor washing.

His toiletries fit into a black leather bag, while mine resembled a burgeoning pharmacy packed in a half-dozen plastic bags.

The next day, while waiting for the bus to take us to Durban and the conference, Lorenzo asked me if he could write about the differences in what we had brought.

He was from Colombia, he explained, a country with exceedingly low emissions. I hail from the United States, the world's second-largest emitter.

Could it be that the differences in what we brought pointed to some differences in consumption?

"It says something," he said after asking my permission to write about my goodies.

I agreed after telling him that his question mirrored my wife's feedback.

Yet, as accurate as he is, my Colombian colleague and friend's total footprint for his conference attendance may well exceed mine. That's because of an area of climate change that thus far has bedeviled even the most creative and innovative of environmentalists: airplanes' enormous consumption of fossil fuels.

Lorenzo told me that his flight took him from his native Colombia to Atlanta, Georgia before flying to Johannesburg and then Durban.

My trip, on the other hand, began in Chicago, continued through Washington, DC, Dakar, Senegal and Johannesburg before boarding the same flight as Lorenzo to Durban.

As a result, then, because of his extra miles, Lorenzo may have the greater carbon footprint for his participation in the conference.

I write this not to explain away the excessive quantity of goods that I brought but rather to raise one of the most fundamental questions running throughout these talks.

Even if the world's nations come to an accord that pledges to reduce the world's emissions to the necessary levels, are we as a global community willing to make the necessary behavioral changes to achieve those goals?

In the world of air travel, the answer is not optimistic.

Despite calls in British activist and author George Monbiot's *Heat* for long-distance air travel to be drastically curtailed, if not completely eliminated, the massive consumption of fossil fuels by flights continues unabated.

This is not to say that the situation is hopeless, but rather to underscore some of the less considered aspects facing the peoples of the world.

In his book, *Science is A Contact Sport*, the late Stephen Schneider, recipient of the 2007 Collective Nobel Peace Prize and one of the key figures for decades in the Intergovernmental Panel on Climate Change, wrote that his students maintained that the contributions he made to the issue outweighed the negative value of his footprint through air travel.

Although I would agree and apply the same reasoning to Lorenzo's participation here, I'm not sure.

But one thing I do know.

The next time I travel anywhere, when it comes time to pack, I'm listening to my wife.

TREEPRENEUR BUSISIWE NDLELA

Dec. 21, 2011

Treepreneur Busisiwe Ndlela.
(Photo by Jeff Kelly Lowenstein)

Busisiwe Ndlela's mother died from asthma in Verulam, South Africa when the girl was just 14 years old.

Busisiwe had never known her father.

Her twin brother had died years before.

Her mother's death left her alone in the world.

But before her passing, her mother imparted a valuable lesson.

"You must depend on yourself," Ndlela, who looks younger than her 60 years, said her mother told her. "You must work hard."

"From that day I worked hard to today," she said.

Ndlela first worked for her mother's employer, raising that woman's children for six years.

She then moved to a long-term stint with a family in suburban Durban North. In her second job, she cared for that family's children, and then for the parents as they aged.

Since 2008, though, Ndlela, whose name means, "The road where we are," has turned her unwavering work ethic to planting trees.

About 1,200 of them.

Ndlela is one more than 600 "treepreneurs" in the Buffelsdraai area northwest of Durban who have been working with conservation non-profit Wildlands Conservation Trust on an innovative pilot program that seeks to restore a 2000-acre sugar cane field to its original state.

In so doing, the program seeks to educate residents about climate change, provide a much-needed boost to the local economy and become an eco-tourist destination.

The City of Durban purchased the property from sugar cane company Tongaat-Hulett prior to the program's start in 2008.

Richard Winn, environmental manager at Durban Solid Waste, the city's waste management department, explained that the project gives interested people trees to plant from seeds that have gathered in the area. His department supplies topsoil to program participants.

The amount of payment a treepreneur receives depends on the height of the tree.

A tree that is 1 foot tall pays 5 rand, or about 60 cents.

A 20-inch tree pays 7.50, or about 90 cents.

A tree that is about one yard high pays 10 rand, or $1.25.

The money has been a welcome addition for treepreneur Ziningi Gcabashe.

One of the program's original participants, she has gone on to plant more than 15,000 trees. She's used the money from the trees to pay for items like her children's school fees.

Gcabashe said the program has grown in popularity since people have seen its success. Learning how to plant trees has also helped people do their part to combat climate change, she said.

Winn said that the trees are the first step in a three-stage process that will take place over several years as about 250 acres per year are altered.

Subsequent steps include having the treepreneurs shift to being "super growers" who work on planting second-level plants to achieve a higher level of biodiversity.

The third stage will involve hiring area residents to maintain the altered landscape.

As the metropolitan Durban area's largest forest, Buffelsdraai could supply trees for people in the surrounding 30 miles, according to Winn.

He said it also could become an eco-tourism and residential destination.

"When they've got 800 hectares of forest doing its cleaning, people will want to move in," he said.

Sean O'Donoghue, acting manager of Durban's climate protection branch, said the potential jobs could inject a new element into the often heated debate between conservationists and those who want to develop the land for commercial purposes.

"This is the first time that conservation brings jobs to people," he said.

Count on Ndlela to be one of the employees.

"It must carry on," she said about the program. "We are not starving."

CECILE MAROTTE'S QUEST TO BRING A PARK TO HAITI

Nov. 23, 2010

One of the many things Dunreith and I love about Evanston is the parks.

There are close to 100 of them in our small city. This number includes one in our backyard that is a rectangle enclosed by a gravel road, the backs of houses and a parking garage. The green space has swings and a field where Aidan and I for years threw the football around after school and on vacations and weekends.

The small park represents more than the total number of such spaces in the entire country of Haiti, but Cecile Marotte and a dedicated group of people are working to change that.

A French native who was trained in the United States in philosophy and ethnopsychiatry, Cecile has lived in Haiti for close to a quarter century. We met during the past two weeks at the Harvard Program in Refugee Trauma.

Cecile and other members have received a four-year grant from the Open Society Institute to design, develop community support for, and oversee construction of the nation's first park.

It is a stiff task.

Haiti has no shortage of issues, including the earthquake that rocked the city in January, the cholera that is wreaking additional havoc and the upcoming elections. Cecile is working in Martissant, a suburb of Port-au-Prince previously known as the "Area of No Rights." Even in one of the world's poorest countries, this community stands out as having no government services.

There are no schools or running water.

Trees grow on garbage.

And murder is common.

Cecile and the other workers, all Haitian nationals, have held a series of meetings with a wide range of groups in the community. This includes gang leaders, who said they would like to create the park. Each meeting is recorded and minutes are distributed to all who have attended.

The ultimate vision is to create a safe and beautiful space monitored by gunless guards where people can visit, chat and tell their stories. In so doing, they have the potential to help the community heal from its many wounds, create the basis to push for greater levels of justice and even contribute to reducing violence.

Sudhir Venkatesh wrote in *Off The Books* about the challenges and compromises that often accompany working with gang leaders, and Cecile is well aware of them. Still, to me there is something compelling about this plan, which is like a shoot growing up the cracks of cement, vulnerable to being crushed yet containing within it the seed of transformative beauty.

I'll let you know about what I learn as the project progresses. In the meantime, I will walk around Evanston with Dunreith and an even greater appreciation of our green spaces.

NEMIA TEMPORAL'S TEARS FOR REFUGEE MOTHERS

Nov. 30, 2010

My two weeks in Orvieto, Italy at the Harvard Program in Refugee Trauma provided plenty of memorable moments.

One of the most vivid came during a lecture on the subject of attachment.

The professor was an elderly Italian gentleman who showed us a clip of a mother breast-feeding a three-month-old baby in her home, then another clip of the baby nine months later. He explained that there had been violence in the home in the intervening time and pointed out that the now older child demonstrated less attached behavior than he had before.

The video and the direction of the presentation elicited a lot of comment and frustration. Some group members expressed dismay that fathers were not included in the study, but the work purported to make general statements about attachment and parenting. Others did not seem to respond well to the professor's answer that some people are made uncomfortable by the sight of mothers breast-feeding their children.

Nemia rose to speak.

A diminutive Filipina who has worked in more than 70 countries during her past quarter century's employment at the United Nations High Commissioner on Refugees, she currently directs a camp in Uganda that holds 130,000 people. Nemia has a disability and walks with great effort and a pronounced limp.

Unfailingly pleasant and humble, she looked almost surprised at the wave of emotion that came over her as she started to speak.

Tears started to pool in her eyes.

Nemia tried in vain to hold them down, then apologized for her lack of composure.

She attempted to speak again.

More tears.

A respectful hush filled the room.

Finally, like a boxer after an eight count, she steadied herself and started to speak.

She spoke about the pain of the mothers who did not eat or drink for a month before arriving at the refugee camp. She talked about how they stagger into the camp, barely alive. And she described their agony at having survived the harrowing ordeal, only to discover that they had no milk with which to feed their children.

Nemia finished her statement, the group clapped in appreciation and the lecture resumed its grinding and ponderous pace.

But the memory of Nemia's compassion remained for me and all who were there and open to receiving the power of the moment.

Long after the memory of the taste of the rabbit and the flush of the fine wine we drank during the course has faded, I'll remember Nemia's empathy and courage, and be grateful I was in the room.

AN ENLIVENING HERITAGE: REINTRODUCING ROBERT COLES

Aug. 4, 2015

NOTE: *I wrote this essay for The Common Review in 2012. Dear friend Danny Postel commissioned and edited the piece.*

Books by Robert Coles discussed in this essay:

Handing One Another Along: Literature and Social Reflection, edited by Trevor Hall and Vicki Kennedy, Random House, 304 pages

Lives We Carry with Us: Profiles of Moral Courage, edited by David D. Cooper, The New Press, 240 pages

To understand Robert Coles' two latest books, it helps to have seen his writing chair.

Comfortable and unassuming, it sits with a blanket draped over it in the study of the three-story house in Concord, Massachusetts, where he and his late wife, Jane, raised their three boys.

The wall opposite the chair features a gallery of framed black-and-white photographs of his personal heroes, many of whom appear in his books—here is William Carlos Williams, there is Walker Percy, and there, in the bottom row, is a smiling Bruce Springsteen, his arm around Coles' shoulder, like a brother. The chair is where Coles has sat and written, on long sheets of yellow lined paper, dozens of books including volumes of poetry, a novel, and books for children and adults, as well as more than 1,000 scholarly articles and reviews.

It was in that chair that Coles wrote the books that made him a major public intellectual in the 1960s and 1970s, before the term was in use. *Children of Crisis*, a five-volume series, remains perhaps his most famous work. The series examines the moral and spiritual lives of children across the country with a poignancy that struck a deep chord in the culture. (In 1973 Coles received the Pulitzer Prize for Volumes Two and Three).

During those years Coles also worked as a speechwriter for Robert Kennedy, crafting the senator's final speech before his assassination in 1968. But he by no means operated exclusively behind the scenes: his writings appeared in the pages of *Harper's Magazine, The New Yorker,* and the *The Atlantic Monthly*; he could be seen on *The Dick Cavett Show*; and his name and reputation were familiar to a wide swath of Americans.

Coles remained in the chair in the 1980s, when he maintained a prominent public profile. During that decade he received a MacArthur "genius grant," appeared often as a guest on the *PBS NewsHour* (then known simply as *The MacNeil/Lehrer NewsHour*), and delivered an address at Harvard's 350th anniversary.

And he has written in the chair over the past two decades, when, despite continuing to garner some of the nation's highest civilian honors (the National Humanities Medal, among others) and launching and editing the short-lived but critically acclaimed national magazine *DoubleTake*, his public profile began to fade. (Coles received the National Humanities Medal from President George W. Bush in 2001, the same year Johnny Cash won the National Medal of Arts. When I spoke with him, Coles recalled an incredulous Cash asking him before the ceremony at which the president and first lady presented their medals, "What the hell are the two of us doin' here?")

It is precisely because of this relative decline in influence that the publication of Coles' newest books, *Handing One Another Along* and *Lives We Carry with Us*, is so welcome. A distillation of his life's essential themes and relationships, these works represent an opportunity to reintroduce one of America's most significant public intellectuals of recent decades to the public.

Spry and trim, Coles looks much younger in person than his eighty-two years. His face is lined and the stubble underneath his left cheek is gray, but his full crest of hair still has healthy portions of its original black color, and his piercing eyes underneath his thick eyebrows retain plenty of vitality. The day I went to visit Coles at his Concord home, I had to wait for him to return from a spontaneous bike ride he took because he could not resist the glorious New England fall weather. Nevertheless, he knows that he is heading toward the end of his life, and he is starting to reflect on and share what he has learned from his many decades of engagement with the world.

At an initial glance, Coles' two most recent works are very different. Edited by David Cooper, *Lives We Carry with Us* draws on Coles' writing for a variety of books and journals to assemble 13 profiles of lives of moral courage. Coles and Cooper, who worked together to choose the book's selections, divide the work into four sections. The first is about teachers and mentors who had a major impact on Coles' life while the following sections cover artists, people of great moral conviction, and people at the beginning and end of the life cycle. The primary focus in the work is on the subjects' lives, and, to a lesser degree, Coles' relationships with them.

Handing One Another Along, on the other hand, is the book version of a series of lectures about literature and art that Coles gave in his legendary Literature of Social Reflection course at Harvard, which he taught for more than 25 years and which he hoped would be an "enlivening heritage." "I hope that the stories, in sum, told through words and pictures, studied through a lens of our own personal and social reflections, can prompt you to stop and consider the way in which you perceive and interact with the world around you, and how you choose to participate in this one life given to you, to us," he writes in the introduction.

Handing One Another Along is also symphonic in nature, introducing ideas that are later developed and expanded. Readers meet the poet and doctor William Carlos Williams in the book's opening section and then hear his words resonate throughout the work's later parts.

Although the difference in form and format of these two works highlights Coles' considerable versatility, together they constitute a single meditation on the people, themes, method of living, and understanding of life's rhythms that have been most central to him. Many of the people in the picture gallery in Coles' study appear in both books.

Far from making a single point in these books, Coles simultaneously advocates multiple specific messages—be kind, be open, be humble, be adventurous, be reflective, be engaged. Both works also contain a similar insistence on decency, an openness to learning from all different types of people and different forms of creative expression, and Coles' guarding against excessive pride and self-promotion. Both works demonstrate an awareness of the possibilities and limitations of each intellectual discipline or form of communication. And both share a bedrock insistence on the importance of questing for truth, of living with soulful authenticity, and of striving for moral courage.

New England Roots

It all started in the lively Coles household in Boston. His parents read selections from their favorite works of literature aloud. The young Coles witnessed spirited discussions between his mother, Sandra, a Tolstoy devotee (in *Handing One Another Along* he describes his mother reading the Russian novelist on her deathbed), and his father, Philip, who told him, "Bobby, if you've got *Middlemarch*, you don't need anything else."

"My father revered Eliot," Coles told me.

His parents' differences went beyond literary taste. His mother was from Sioux City, Iowa, an artist and art collector. On one of the walls in Coles' home hang original works by Monet, Picasso, and Munch that she purchased. A stark presence is the art of Käthe Kollwitz, which portrays the desperate poverty that wracked post–World War I Germany. "I met the poor through Kollwitz," Coles told me.

An exacting woman, Coles' mother instilled in him an almost instinctive guarding against excessive self-glorification and pride. At times this tendency of his mother's took extreme forms. He told me a story about bringing home a straight-A report card from Boston Latin School. His mother looked at it and said, "At moments like this, Bobby, we have to humble ourselves, and be grateful for the gifts the Lord has given us, but also be aware that there are flaws."

"Your mother's right, but she should give you a break," responded his father, who was in the room and had been listening.

Philip Coles was an MIT-trained engineer of Jewish ancestry who, while an agnostic, derived spiritual pleasure and sustenance from the work of George Eliot and fellow literary rebel Thomas Hardy. Coles' mother came from Episcopalian and Catholic stock. This mixture led Coles away from a decisive belief in a single tradition or even in the existence of God. It also made him open to and sympathetic toward people from each of those religions, though he has never fully subscribed to any of them. "I have always felt between various worlds," he said, a wry smile creasing his face. "Maybe it's motivated me to understand the complexities of other people."

The quest to live with and understand ambiguities through art and writing, the belief that apparent opposites needn't be so, the emphasis on accomplishment and humility, the passion for creative expression, and the need to act with moral courage against poverty and for social justice— all were guiding themes in Coles' childhood experiences and in his mature work.

Coles graduated from Boston Latin and enrolled in Harvard in 1946. Like his brother William, he aspired to a career teaching English and, perhaps, writing. (William taught English literature for many years at the University of Michigan before retiring to Arizona.)

Enter Dr. Williams

William Carlos Williams, the bard of New Jersey, the doctor who made house calls among ordinary citizens for a half-century, writing all the while, was to play a formative role in Coles' life. Williams's footprints are all over *Lives We Carry with Us*, which takes its title from a Williams injunction: "Their story, yours and mine—it's what we all carry with us on this trip we take, and we owe it to each other to respect our stories and learn from them." Coles' incorporation and adaptation of these words is just one of the ways he honors his mentor. Williams is also a key figure in the first section of *Lives We Carry with Us*, in which Coles focuses on five people who exerted a life-altering influence on him.

Williams may stand atop that select list. Coles was introduced to his writing—then mostly ignored by the literary professoriate—by Perry Miller, Coles' undergraduate advisor. Under Miller's guidance, Coles wrote a paper about Williams, but Miller pushed his student to meet the literary master. Coles describes the scene in *Handing One Another Along*:

Professor Miller said to me, "Why don't you send what you've written to Dr. Williams." I said, "What?" He said, "That, what you wrote." I said, "I can't do that." He said, "You don't have the postage? No, you're either shy or embarrassed." I said nothing. He continued: "It might mean something to him."

Coles sent the paper and received a reply from New Jersey about a week later:

"I opened it up and there was a piece of paper from a doctor's small, square prescription pad: William C. Williams, M.D., 9 Ridge Road, Rutherford, New Jersey. The prescription said, "Dear Mr. Coles, thank you very much for sending your thesis to me. It's not bad for a Harvard student." In a new paragraph, he added, "If you are ever in the neighborhood, please come see Flossie and me. Bill."

A week later, Coles writes, he went to New York to be "in the neighborhood." He met Williams and that was it. In *Lives We Carry with Us*, Coles describes Williams' influence: "For me, to know Dr. Williams, to hear him talk about his writing and his life of medical work among the poor and working people of northern New Jersey, was to change direction markedly. Once headed for teaching, I set my sights for medical school."

Application and admission to Columbia Medical School followed. While there, Coles met another mentor, this one courtesy of his mother: Dorothy Day, founder of the Catholic Worker Movement.

Coles' mother had carried on a correspondence with Day, and she shared the connection with her son in typically crisp fashion. During a lecture at Phillips Brooks House, home to a Harvard student organization dedicated to social justice, Coles explained that his mother responded to a description of his academic struggles by saying, "Maybe if you met Dorothy and the people she's working with, you'd stop feeling so sorry for yourself."

The student heeded his mother's advice, and, through meeting Day, started to discover a way that he could be a doctor without neglecting his desire to work for social justice. Like Williams, Day receives a full chapter in *Lives We Carry with Us*, appears in *Handing One Another Along*, and has a portrait in the pantheon on the wall in Coles' study.

In *Lives We Carry with Us*, Coles writes that Day helped him with his struggle to "connect a strong interest in moral philosophy to the work I was learning as a member of a particular profession."

The connection took time. A lot of it. In fact, Coles explained during that same lecture that he spent so much time with Williams and Day that he was summoned to the dean's office. Failing to concentrate more fully on his medical studies, they said, could jeopardize his completion of them.

Coles buckled down sufficiently to graduate. In part because of his encounters with Anna Freud (Sigmund's daughter) and her work, the subject of another chapter in *Lives We Carry with Us*, he decided to specialize in child psychiatry.

Heading South

Williams and Miller both urged Coles not to stay in academia, but to get outside its gates and see the world. Recently married to the former Jane Hallowell, Coles was fortunate that his bride not only acquiesced, but supported the exploration. Their travels took them south to Keesler Air Force Base in Biloxi, Mississippi, where Coles served as a military psychiatrist.

While in Mississippi, Coles traveled to New Orleans and witnessed what he calls in *Handing One Another Along* "an incident that transformed my life, my work, my perspective, the trajectory of my career." The incident was a riot outside William Frantz Elementary School in New Orleans. Having grown up in the North, Coles had not had direct contact with segregation and the venomous hatred that could be stirred when its order was threatened. (The brutal response in South Boston to Judge Arthur Garrity's court-ordered school desegregation of Boston's public schools by busing took place close to 15 years after the upheaval Coles witnessed.)

Coles describes the scene in *Handing One Another Along*:

Once I got within sight of the school, I saw, as well as heard, a large group of people, and all kinds of shouting and screaming. Then, almost suddenly, I saw some cars drive up, and if you have ever heard a noisy, foulmouthed mob suddenly fall silent, you will know the noise of silence, the presence of silence.

Men got out of the first car, all dressed alike in gray flannel suits, sunglasses, and carrying guns. A couple of men got out of the second car, but they didn't have guns at the ready—rather, they were holding on to a little girl, who was about four feet tall and had on a white dress, white shoes, a white bow in her hair and was carrying a lunch pail.

After the silence came the noise again, the screams, the shouts, the threats: "We are going to kill you, you blankety-blankety-blank."

The girl was six-year-old Ruby Bridges, a black girl who was integrating the previously all-white school. The protestors' rage shocked the sheltered Coles, who had slowly begun "to figure out that this had to do with race," and sparked in him the curiosity to learn more and a determination to find out what was happening. After meeting with NAACP Legal Defense Fund chief Thurgood Marshall, Coles gained permission to meet and work with Bridges.

A chapter in each of the two books is devoted to his relationship with Bridges. In *Handing One Another Along*, Coles says that he asked what she was doing when she moved her lips each morning. She was praying, the girl told him. Coles then asked,

"Who are you praying for?" She replied, "I was praying for the people in the street." I was surprised and unwilling to drop the matter. I said, "Why would you want to pray for those people in the street?" She looked at me and answered, "Well, don't you think they need praying for? I always say the same thing. I always say, 'Please God, try to forgive these people because they don't know what they are doing.'"

The hatred he witnessed in the South confused Coles, and made him feel lonely and adrift. A partial antidote came in the form of Walker Percy's novel *The Moviegoer*. Coles writes in *Lives We Carry with Us* that he had read Percy's essays for years, adding that when *The Moviegoer* came out in 1961, he read it so many times he lost count. The book "gave hope to me, helped me feel stronger at a critical time, when I was somewhat lost, confused, vulnerable, and, it seemed, drifting badly."

The exchange with Bridges and the reliance on Percy's work illustrate the spiritual and religious understanding that took shape during Coles' childhood and which he made his own. Coles believes we live in a moral universe in which right and wrong do exist and matter. Striving for moral courage is desirable and honorable, if not imperative. Like his father, Coles drew strength from literature rather than organized religion or personal belief.

While he is deeply respectful of others' faith in God, Coles himself does not have that same certainty. "I just don't know," he said after I asked him about the topic for the third time in his study. "I'm an agnostic."

Bolstered by Percy's work and by his relationship with Williams, Coles stayed with his family in the South for more than a decade, becoming heavily involved in the burgeoning civil rights struggle that toppled legal segregation.

It was dangerous work.

Coles told me that he was in the same car as civil rights workers James Chaney, Michael Schwerner, and Andrew Goodman in Mississippi the evening of Sunday, June 21, 1964. The men were going to investigate the burning of Mount Zion Union Methodist Church, fifty miles away in Neshoba County.

Coles was planning to ride with the three men, but the legendary organizer Bob Moses, who was staying to attend a meeting in the area, intervened.

"Bob Moses came over and put his hand on my shoulder and he said, 'You're a white American Harvard doctor. They'll listen to you, they won't listen to me.'"

Coles got out of the car and went with Moses.

Schwerner, Chaney, and Goodman disappeared that night. The next day their burned-out station wagon was found in the Bogue Chitto swamp. The bodies of the three civil rights workers were found 44 days later, buried 15 feet in an earthen dam.

Philip Coles was furious at his son for staying in such perilous conditions, especially with his wife pregnant with their first child; but Coles and Jane did not leave for several more years. Their next stop was a return to Cambridge and his alma mater, where the psychologist Erik Erikson, yet another towering figure in both books, had invited him to teach.

Coles' years in the South did more than expand his racial horizons, lay the groundwork for the monumental *Children of Crisis*, and give him a visceral awareness of life's fragility. It also inculcated in Coles a deep desire to travel to new places and learn what he could from children's and adults' struggles to act bravely in an often harsh and unfair world. He, his wife, and their three sons ventured to Alaska, where he worked with native people, to apartheid-era South Africa, and to the former Rhodesia among other places.

Out in the World

The Coles family also traveled to the Southwest to work with migrant workers, during which time Coles befriended the legendary farmworker organizer César Chávez. Coles also met an elderly Mexican couple in New Mexico who had been married for more than 60 years. He writes about the pair in "Una Anciana," a chapter in *Lives We Carry With Us* and his favorite piece of writing ever. The book's longest chapter, "Una Anciana" is the only piece in the book to appear in its original version.

Whereas other chapters in *Lives We Carry with Us* feature more standard profile elements—the subjects' backgrounds, formative influences, and biographical milestones—"Una Anciana" transports the reader into the couple's home and gives the woman and her husband much more space to speak for themselves.

"Una Anciana" ends with the husband's tribute to the woman with whom he has shared his life:

She is not just an old woman, you know. She wears old age like a bunch of fresh-cut flowers. She is old, advanced in years, vieja, but in Spanish we have another word for her, a word which tells you that she has grown with all those years. I think that is something one ought hope for and pray for and work for all during life: to grow, to become not only older but a bigger person. She is old, all right, vieja, but I will dare say this in front of her—she is una anciana; with that I declare my respect and have to hurry back to the barn.

The praise could easily have been Coles' words about his own wife, who died in 1993. The excerpt is just one of many passages throughout *Lives We Carry with Us* and *Handing One Another Along* in which Coles, although writing about other people, is speaking about himself. In *Lives We Carry with Us*, for instance, he describes Erik Erikson's search for human understanding as "an unashamedly moral one"—a characterization that could just as easily apply to Coles' own quest. When he writes in *Handing One Another Along* that through the people we meet in William Carlos Williams's work and the "questions that he brings up for us about them, we learn of a nation, its people," we hear echoes of Coles' own intention.

There is a certain irony in this since Coles scrupulously avoids writing positively about himself in both works. When he does appear, he is usually being lovingly corrected by his wife; being educated by the people he meets; or, when he uses psychological terminology, cut down by himself for doing so, often with parenthetical phrases. In one particularly striking example of the latter, he uses three sets of parentheses in the same paragraph! It's a deliberate technique, he told me, to avoid using his authority as a psychologist and doctor to intimidate others. There is also his adherence to his mother's childhood injunction against what George Eliot called "unreflecting egoism."

These tactics notwithstanding, throughout both books Coles sends clear messages about his understanding of life: living incrementally and by the moment, learning as you go, and never acting with utter certainty. Books and literature and art can be guides for action and sources of strength, but one must live life on the ground.

A Controversy

Coles has received multiple honors for his work and methods, ranging from a MacArthur "genius grant" in 1981 to the Presidential Medal of

Freedom, the nation's top honor for civilians, in 1998. But the acclaim has not been unanimous as Coles and his work have come under criticism on a number of grounds. Some have noted that the statements his subjects make are precisely those that a liberal Northern psychiatrist would want to hear. Others have taken direct aim at Coles' credibility and veracity. In a 2003 *New Republic* review of his book about Bruce Springsteen (the subject of one of the profiles in *Lives We Carry with Us*), author David Hajdu wrote the following:

> *The fact that William Carlos Williams and Walker Percy had such extensive conversations with Robert Coles on the subjects of the New Jersey pop singers Frank Sinatra and Bruce Springsteen, and that those discussions yielded insights so parallel and neatly suited to Coles' own take on Springsteen is incredible—utterly incredible. I was not there to overhear them, of course, and it is impossible to check with Williams and Percy, or with the late Erikson and Shawn, whom Coles' other deceased sources quote in his book's opening sections. But I did ask Will Percy about the comments on Springsteen that Coles attributes to his uncle, and he called them "outrageous." Walker Percy "definitely didn't talk like that," according to his nephew.*

Coles, who had a book dedicated to him by Percy, has never commented publicly on the nephew's allegation. He declined to break his silence for this article other than to say that his complete correspondence with Percy and Springsteen is at Michigan State.

On the other hand, he did plead guilty to a criticism, leveled in the mid-1980s by Northwestern professor and social commentator Joseph Epstein, that he is too easy on others' books when he reviews them. "Generosity, like humility, can be carried too far," Epstein wrote in *Plausible Prejudices*. "Doris Grumbach, Robert Coles, and Robert Towers are three people who review too generously. Their liking a book carries no weight—they like so many."

"I have never been able to write negative, nasty reviews," Coles told me, explaining that he instead declines invitations to review books about which he does not have much positive to say. "[Joseph Epstein] is onto something."

Grappling with Life's Mysteries

When it comes to his books, Coles writes with urgency because he knows that his remaining days are limited. He writes poignantly in *Lives We Carry with Us* that a failing Dorothy Day tried, but was unable, to "write what mattered most" to her. In his latest work, Coles does exactly that type of taking stock. In "Una Anciana," when the husband says, "These days one never knows when the end will come. I know our time is soon up. But when I look at that mother horse and her child in the barn, or at my children and their children, I feel lucky to have been permitted for a while to be part of all this life here on earth," one feels Coles' awareness of his own mortality.

Coles develops this theme of gratitude more explicitly in *Handing One Another Along*, with writing from and about authors who faced their deaths with serenity and grace. In a lecture early in that book, he includes Raymond Carver's poem "Gravy," which, according to Coles, describes in many ways "his [Carver's] last decade, a decade of blessedness and love that became possible for him" when Carver quit drinking and began his relationship with writer Tess Gallagher in 1978:

"No other word will do. For that's what it was. Gravy.
Gravy, these past ten years.
Alive, sober, working, loving, and
being loved by a good woman. Eleven years
ago he was told he had six months to live
at the rate he was going. And he was going
nowhere but down. So he changed his ways
somehow. He quit drinking! And the rest?
After that, it was all gravy, every minute
of it, up to and including when he was told about,
well, some things that were breaking down and
building up inside his head. "Don't weep for me,"
he said to his friends. "I'm a lucky man.
I've had ten years longer than I or anyone
expected. Pure Gravy. And don't forget it."

Building on the theme of gratitude touched on by Domingo and Carver, the final chapter of *Handing One Another Along* contains Jane Kenyon's poem "Otherwise," which she wrote shortly before she died of leukemia at age forty-eight:

I got out of bed
on two strong legs.
It might have been
otherwise. I ate
cereal, sweet
milk, ripe, flawless
peach. It might
have been otherwise.
I took the dog uphill
to the birch wood.
All morning I did
the work I love.

At noon I lay down
with my mate. It might
have been otherwise.
We ate dinner together
at a table with silver
candlesticks. It might
have been otherwise.
I slept in a bed
in a room with paintings
on the walls, and
planned another day
just like this day.
But one day, I know,
it will be otherwise.

"How does one live with such knowledge?" Coles asks. "How to pick up each day with enthusiasm and insistence and pride and yet know, remember what that poem tells us?"

Coles' answer, it seems, lies in the words of a letter Henry James wrote to his nephew, William, that Coles includes in the final chapter of *Handing One Another Along*, and in the values by which Coles has oriented his personal and professional life: Be kind. Be brave. Be open. Be respectful. Be hard working. Be humble. Be honest. Be true.

Next

It might be reasonable to expect that, having shared his life's wisdom, Coles has no plans for more books. But that is not the case. Next on the docket is a return to the beginning of his career in medicine, when he cared for children with polio and other fatal conditions (*Handing One Another Along* contains a reference to the same period in Coles' life). During the October lecture at Phillips Brooks House, he recounted how one of the children told him, "You look tired, Dr. Coles." The suffering child's compassionate gesture lives within the psychiatrist still and is prodding him to explore that territory.

Before that though, there are bike rides to take, letters to write, and family members to visit. He said he considers his relationship with his wife and family his greatest accomplishment.

But when he has rested and readied himself, Robert Coles will sit back in his trusty chair. He will take out another pad of yellow lined paper. And, in the shadows of the people who have meant most to him and inspired these two books, he will begin to carry out the next, and what we hope is not the final, project of his extraordinarily rich, varied, and productive life.

ACKNOWLEDGMENTS

This book is a testament to the truth that nobody does anything significant on his own. While I bear full responsibility for any errors and the work itself, I've had tremendous support along the way.

The first thanks must go to Fernando Diaz. We both worked at *The Chicago Reporter* in December 2008. I was talking with him about Beauty Turner's sudden and devastating death.

"So, are you going to write about it in your blog?" he responded.

Fernando's challenge moved me to carry out what I had talked about but had yet to do: blog on a regular basis. After I got started he helped me understand how to cultivate and sustain a community.

Top commenters and boosters like Paul Tamburello, Jack Crane, David Russell, Derrick Milligan, Lynn Ochberg and Bob Yovovich have been critical parts of that community. Their response and affirmation have helped me have faith in the impact of what I was doing. Dan Middleton has been both an active contributor and an occasional guest blogger.

In addition to writing his generous introduction, Danny Postel has been a constant source of ideas, encouragement and companionship. I am grateful to him for all of his gifts.

It's been a great source of joy and meaning to collaborate for more than a decade in a myriad of way with Jon Lowenstein, my brother and a decorated photographer. I'm grateful that his images are some of the ones that appear in this book and to all of the other photographers who have let me use their work. This group consists of Tom Kates, Genevieve Lee of TrueLee Photography, John Moore, Mohamad Ojjeh and Poul Rasmussen.

Javier Suárez did impressive work on the design in what I'm confident will be the first project in an ongoing relationship.

Ava Kadishson Schieber is one of the wisest, most knowledgeable and creative people I've ever met. I continue to learn from how she wrings every ounce of experience possible out of her life and am appreciative of her willingness to allow me to put her artwork on the book's cover.

Like all major projects in my life, my family has given me unconditional love and support. To give just one example, I was thrilled to see a lengthy and thoughtful comment to one of my very first posts–and only slightly less excited to read, "Love, Dad" at the end of it.

Two people in particular played a vital role in this project. Ginna Freed spent countless hours reading and editing every word of the entries that make up this volume as well as others that did not make the final edition. It's a gift I can never fully repay. It is to her this volume is dedicated.

In the spring of 2000, I was living in Boston and feeling discouraged after not having gained admission to graduate programs in writing.

Dunreith, who was living with Aidan in the western part of the state, told me, "You can come out here and write."

So I did.

Much has happened since Fernando pushed me to make good on my stated intention.

We've had moments of joy like Aidan's graduations from high school and college. My brother Mike and his wife Annie got married and a year later welcomed their son Matthew into the world. We've returned with Dad to his hometown in Germany for the first time in 73 years and celebrated the completion of two books.

We've endured losses as well as we've continued moving along the path of life.

My stepmother Diane Lowenstein and mother's cousin Gary Adelman have died.

So have my beloved in-laws, Helen and Marty Kelly, and treasured and inspiring activists Beauty Turner and Becky Simpson.

President Obama has taken office and served the majority of his two terms as the nation's first black president.

Despite vitriolic rhetoric that compared him to Adolf Hitler, he ushered through the passage of the Affordable Care Act – a landmark law that has been affirmed twice by the Supreme Court that includes Sonia Sotomayor, the institution's first Latina.

Our nation seems more polarized than ever, and climate change's devastating effects have become more apparent.

During the time I have maintained the blog, its focus shifted from writing about books to daily sources of joy to our adventures in Chile.

But what remained constant and indeed even increased was the pleasure and meaning I got from sitting down to express what was inside of me at that moment and share it with the world. This blog has been an important space for me to continue to develop my writing voice and life sensibility in a collective space. Thank you for engaging with the posts along the way and for taking some of your precious time and energy to read this collection of my favorites here.

ABOUT THE AUTHOR

Jeff Kelly Lowenstein was born in Brookline, Mass. in 1965 and has loved writing for many years. He and his wife Dunreith live in Evanston, Illinois. Their son Aidan graduated from Tulane University in May 2015. This is Kelly Lowenstein's third book.

NOTES

40107171R00162

Made in the USA
Middletown, DE
03 February 2017